OUR SISTERS
IN THE
LATTER-DAY
SCRIPTURES

OUR SISTERS
IN THE
LATTER-DAY
SCRIPTURES

JERRIE W. HURD

Deseret Book Company
Salt Lake City, Utah

First printing September 1987

Library of Congress Cataloging-in-Publication Data

Hurd, Jerrie W.
    Our sisters in the latter-day Scriptures.

    Includes index.
    1. Mormon Church—Sacred books—Biography.   2. Church
of Jesus Christ of Latter-day Saints—Sacred books
—Biography.   3. Women, Mormon—Biography.   I. Title.
BX8622.H87   1987   289.3'2'088042   87-15619
ISBN 0-87579-091-7

To Jon
and my sisters Karen, Sharen, Becky, and Janet

Contents

Preface

At first it may seem that not many women have been included in the Book of Mormon, Doctrine and Covenants, and Pearl of Great Price, and that those who are included are only mentioned in passing. But fortunately that first impression is wrong. The latter-day scriptures include many womanly examples. To see them you have to focus on them, but it's worth the effort.

While it is true that the latter-day scriptures have fewer references to women than the Bible has, and no stories told in as great detail as those of Ruth and Esther, the quality of the references is more pervasive, giving a greater sense of how women have influenced all aspects of life, both for good and for evil. That is not an insignificant consideration.

By contrast the quality of the womanly examples in some other histories is not as uplifting. Great literature provides many images of women—some flattering, some not, and some that seem flattering but are not helpful. For example, take Helen of Troy. She has been described as "the face that launched a thousand ships." From that description we can assume that she was beautiful, but beauty is superficial and not something an individual woman can always possess. Yet from the Homeric epic on down through the ages, almost nothing else about Helen of Troy is told—little of what she did, less of how she acted, and nothing of how she felt about the war of which she was the central object.

The references to women in the latter-day scriptures may also be brief, but they are meaningful. Women today can relate to Sariah following her husband into the wilderness and Abish preaching to her people and Vienna Jaques giving the Church all her worldly wealth. The heights that women can attain are clearly delineated, as are the faults, weaknesses, and sins that can overcome and destroy them. The latter-day scriptures are faithful records with little romantic idealism in the portraits presented.

Reading the scriptures with the purpose of noticing the women is universally beneficial. In their Church responsibilities, men often find themselves counseling women and girls. Being able to use one example such as Sariah or Abish or the daughters of Onitah can give substance to the advice offered. On the other hand, for some women the scriptures are more difficult to understand because of the general emphasis on men and men's activities. They can sympathize with Mormon's moral dilemma when he was asked to assume the leadership of a wicked nation or with the complexity of Joseph Smith's many challenges, yet at the same time they may feel removed—at arm's length—because they cannot see themselves in those masculine roles. These women need the sense of identity with the scriptures that they can get by looking for references to women and trying to see the events from a woman's point of view. Terms like *wife, mother, sister,* and so forth are easy to overlook, but noting them can round out the picture of what the women and families were doing during all the battles and migrations. Discovering the women in sacred texts can give some women entree, a place to begin a study of the scriptures. For others it can keep in perspective the fact that God works through families more often than through kings or captains.

All of the prophets have urged women to know their

importance and the power of their influence. President Ezra Taft Benson observed, "Adam and Eve . . . labored together; they had children together; they prayed together; and they taught their children the gospel together." When speaking to the women's fireside of the Church in 1979, President Spencer W. Kimball encouraged women to become "sister scripturians." He was simply reiterating what prophets and the written scriptures have encouraged women to become, whenever and wherever the gospel of Jesus Christ has been taught. (See Alma 32:23; D&C 25:7–8; Moses 5:12.)

Women are and always have been closely associated with the unfolding purposes of God. Think of it this way: a woman brought mortality into the world, a woman brought the Savior into the world, and a woman was the first to see the resurrected Christ.

No allowance for differences in time and place need be made. The daughters of Eve today have needs and possibilities as great as those of any of the women mentioned in scripture. *Our Sisters in the Latter-day Scriptures* is offered in the belief that sisters in these latter days will enjoy discovering for themselves their own scriptural heritage.

1
Women in the Book of Mormon

F ew women are named in the Book of Mormon, a fact others have noted before. Often overlooked, however, is the fact that though largely anonymous, women's accomplishments, together with their power and influence, are repeatedly acknowledged by Book of Mormon writers in a way few other ancient records can match.

The Book of Mormon, as a history, focuses on what happened to the descendants of Nephi. Even in retelling those events, none of the ancient writers claimed to be complete. (See Jacob 1:2.) They selected and shortened. Some frankly acknowledged the difficulty of writing anything at all. (See Jarom 1:14.) Some, because of the difficulty of writing on metal plates, wrote fewer than a dozen words to cover years of their nation's history. (See Omni 1:9.) This brief record was then abridged, making it even briefer—Mormon said he could include less than a hundredth of the material he had available. (See Words of Mormon.) Mormon's abridgment of an already brief record was then translated to become the volume of scripture now embraced by The Church of Jesus Christ of Latter-day Saints. Given all that condensation and abbreviation, the marvel is not that so few women are included but that such a rich concern for women should have survived to color large portions of the Book of Mormon, beginning with the opening passage.

Sariah and the Other Women in the Wilderness

Sariah is one of the "goodly" parents her son Nephi honored in the first verse of the Book of Mormon. If examined from her point of view, the narrative that follows can be said to center on her family: her husband's visions; her sons' expeditions and dissensions; her brother's family joining their exodus; her own struggles and spiritual growth; and the children born to her in the wilderness. Her influence is subtle, yet it is woven into every part of the story. It can be easily overlooked, yet it was not underestimated by those writing the record. Whenever her son Nephi counted his blessings, he always included his mother and the other women who were with him in the wilderness—at least nine of them.

Sariah found herself rearing a family in difficult times. On the surface she seems well-favored: she was a wealthy matron living in Jerusalem, a city bustling with people and commerce, a city often visited by kings and queens of other nations. All was not well in Jerusalem, however. Except for Josiah, unrighteous kings had ruled Judah. Idolatry was rampant. Statues of Baal stood in the temple itself (see Jeremiah 32:34), and the Assyrian worship of stars and planets had been introduced into the city. The scriptures testify that many men and women with spiritual insight were alarmed. Several prophets—Habakkuk, Zephaniah, Jeremiah, Uriah, and Lehi—and one prophetess—Huldah—had warned the people that their great city would be destroyed if they did not repent. But their warnings went unheeded. A school of professional "prophets" had been established, and these men and women were artful in delivering comforting, flattering messages. They persuaded the people that the warnings of God's true prophets were uninspired and unpatriotic. Several of those prophets suffered abuse. Jeremiah was imprisoned, and the life of Lehi, Sariah's husband, was threatened. Being warned by God, he took his family and fled.

There is a consistent theme in the Old Testament of the prophets consulting with their wives and listening to them, even of being told by God to do so. It was true of Adam and Eve, Abraham and Sarah, Isaac and Rebekah, and others. Several passages in the Book of Mormon seem to suggest that Lehi and Sariah fit into that tradition. Lehi probably discussed his plans with Sariah before they left Jerusalem. How she received his ideas is not recorded, but her courage suggests that she acted out of conviction. Seemingly she agreed; if not readily, then gradually, as through her own efforts she came to a testimony that what they were doing was right.

Several years after Lehi and Sariah's departure, Nebuchadnézzar besieged Jerusalem. For eighteen months his army strangled the city. Hunger became so acute that children were eaten. When the city surrendered, all high officials and leading professionals were marched outside the city and executed. Lehi would surely have been one of those. Others were herded together and taken into exile in Babylon. The walls were leveled, and everything else was burned.

By leaving, Sariah and her family escaped this fate, but she did not have that historical perspective when she made her decision. She had only a husband who was a "visionary man" and the Lord's promise, through Lehi, that he would lead her family to a choice land. Nevertheless she seems to have gone willingly, leaving behind a life of ease for the rigors of the wilderness.

Once in the desert, Lehi was directed in a dream to send his sons back to Jerusalem for the brass plates of Laban. That was not a task to be taken lightly. There was a great distance to traverse, and then getting the plates meant undertaking delicate negotiations—if the plates could be obtained at all. The plates of Laban contained Lehi's genealogy and a record of God's dealings with the Israelites. The Lord did not want Lehi and his descendants to dwindle in unbelief for the lack of a written account of the doctrines and practices of the true religion. Understandably, Lehi's sons received the command to return for the brass plates with mixed feelings. Laman and Lemuel felt it was a hard task. Nephi agreed but expressed his faith that the Lord would not require anything without also providing a way to accomplish it.

Seemingly Sariah did not enter that controversy until her sons' return was long overdue. Then, out of motherly concern, she complained. Thinking that her sons had perished, she mourned, berating Lehi for his dreams, telling him that his visions would be the death of them all.

Lehi's response is typical of the concern for women that is shown in the Book of Mormon. Without belittling her worries, Lehi agreed with her that he was a "visionary man" and then gave his witness of the things he had seen, the "things of God" and the "goodness of God." (1 Nephi 5:4-6.) He assured her their sons would be delivered out of the hands of Laban and would return to them. The account suggests that this was not a single incident, that Lehi comforted Sariah again and again as they anxiously waited.

When Nephi and his brothers finally returned with the plates, Sariah was moved to express her own testimony. She said, "Now I know of a surety that the Lord hath commanded my husband to flee into the wilderness; yea, and I also know of a surety that the Lord hath protected my sons, and delivered them out of the hands of Laban, and given them power whereby they could accomplish the thing which the Lord hath commanded them." (1 Nephi 5:8.) Then "they," meaning Lehi and Sariah, offered sacrifices and gave thanks to the Lord, indicating that Sariah took part in those religious observances.

Lehi sent his sons back to Jerusalem yet another time. On the second trip, Nephi and his brothers asked Ishmael and his family to join them in their journey, and he did, promptly following them into the desert with his large household. Ishmael's relationship to Lehi is not given in the Book of Mormon. The account tells in some detail about Zoram, the servant of Laban who chose to follow Nephi and his brothers into the desert when his master was killed; but in writing about this incident, Nephi takes Ishmael completely for granted, never explaining who he is. The act of sending for him seems to have been the most natural thing in the world, as does the marriage of his daughters to Lehi's sons. His casual introduction into the narrative and the fact that marriage between near relatives was the norm for this culture strongly suggest a family connection.

Many scholars consider it likely that Ishmael's sons were already married to Sariah's daughters. This assumption is based on a speech Elder Erastus Snow gave in 1882 in which he quoted Joseph Smith as saying that Ishmael's sons had married into Lehi's family. (See *Journal of Discourses*, 23:184.) Indeed, Ishmael's sons already have families when they are first introduced in the text. (See 1 Nephi 7:6.)

Considering this close family connection and the fact that Sariah had expressed her testimony that what they were doing was directed by God, the second time she waited for her sons to return, her anxieties were probably different. Convinced of the imminent destruction of Jerusalem, as expressed in her testimony, she must have worried that her brother and her daughters might not leave—might not believe and be saved.

If so, her worries were justified. As with the task of returning for the plates, returning for Ishmael's family was not without incident. Laman and Lemuel, who had earlier rebelled against leaving Jerusalem, now found allies in two of Ishmael's daughters, two of Ishmael's sons, and their families.

The Woman Who Saved Nephi's Life

Ishmael, his wife, and three of his daughters sided with Nephi but were unable to help him when his brothers grew violent. Laman and Lemuel overpowered Nephi, bound him, and threatened to take his life. The Lord gave Nephi strength to burst his bonds, but his brothers were so angry that they continued to strive with him until one of Ishmael's daughters, aided by her mother and one of their brothers, pleaded for him. One wonders what she said, for she not only prevented a murder, but she also moved Nephi's brothers to beg forgiveness on bended knee. (See 1 Nephi 7:19–21.)

This conflict points out the divisions among the family members leaving Jerusalem for America. The group now included Lehi and Sariah and their four sons; Zoram, formerly Laban's servant; and Ishmael, his wife, and their five daughters and three sons. (See 1 Nephi 7:6, 19.) Two of Ishmael's sons are said to have had families, their wives being Lehi's daughters. Each of these people was forced by the violent struggle between Nephi and his brothers to decide whether to believe that leaving Jerusalem was inspired. Nothing less would do. Laman and Lemuel had refused to be convinced even by the appearance of an angel. Sariah had struggled, but she came to express her firm testimony. Nephi had asked for and received a confirmation of his father's vision, and at least one of Ishmael's daughters believed—the girl who would become Nephi's wife, who had spoken eloquently in his behalf.

That division of the family is echoed in Lehi's vision of the tree of life. In his vision Lehi partook of the fruit, and his soul was filled with great joy. He looked around for his family, wanting to share his joy with them. He saw Sariah and two of his sons a short way off. He beckoned to them and called with a loud voice, and they came to him and partook of the fruit of the tree. Then Lehi looked for Laman and Lemuel and saw them near the head of the river, but they would not come to him. The vision then expanded, and Lehi saw numerous concourses of people pressing toward the tree, most of whom were lost in the mists clouding the way, some becoming ashamed and joining the men and women mocking from a great, spacious building, and others entering forbidden paths or being drowned in the river.

That vision caused Lehi to despair over Laman and Lemuel, and Sariah must have shared that anxiety. How does a mother react to division and hostility among her children? Indications are that Sariah continued to love both the wayward and the upright but placed her hope in the righteous.

The sons of Lehi married the daughters of Ishmael. Zoram, who had formerly been Laban's servant but who proved himself loyal to Nephi, married the eldest of Ishmael's daughters. Nephi explains that in performing these marriages, his father fulfilled all that the Lord had commanded him and again counted himself blessed because of these women.

As if in acknowledgment of that faithfulness, a compass, described as a brass ball of curious workmanship with two spindles, was given to the group by the Lord shortly after the marriages. Taking provisions and seeds, the camp traveled south-southeast following the direction indicated by one of the spindles on the device. They traveled in this way for some time, the ball directing them to the more fertile parts of the wilderness, where the men obtained game with their bows and arrows. Then Nephi broke his bow. Without it he was unable to provide game, and the camp went hungry. The scriptures say that the families "did suffer much for want of food," reinforcing the concern for families the Book of Mormon expresses over and over again.

Nephi made a new bow and asked his father to inquire of the Lord where he should go to find game. Suddenly writing appeared on the ball, astounding the whole camp. At this point Nephi mentions the women specifically and explains that the brass ball, called "Liahona," worked according to faith and that all members of the camp, young and old, men and women, bore responsibility for maintaining the spiritual tenor necessary to receive direction from this device. Following the Liahona's instructions, Nephi obtained food, which was received with great rejoicing, especially, he notes, by the women with young children.

The hunger and hardship these women shared is graphically described after the death of Ishmael. His daughters mourned over the loss of their father and also over their other afflictions. Nephi wrote: "We did travel and wade through much affliction in the wilderness; and our women did bear children in the wilderness," and then he went on to count as a blessing the strength of those women, saying, "So great were the blessings of the Lord upon us, that while we did live upon raw meat in the wilderness, our women did give plenty of suck for their children, and were strong, yea, even like unto the men . . . " He goes on to suggest that their faith and endurance grew. Laman and Lemuel never stopped complaining. But Nephi says of the women, " . . . and they began to bear their journeyings without murmuring." (1 Nephi 17:1-2.) These women bearing children were not just the young wives of Nephi and his brothers. Sariah gave birth to two sons and at least two daughters in the wilderness, "suffering [as Nephi wrote] all things, save it were death," along with the other women.

Nephi constantly speaks of the women with high praise and of his mother with great respect. Once when Nephi was called on to rebuke his brothers by stretching out his arm to jolt them with the power of God, they would have worshipped him, but he forbade it, saying that they should worship God and honor their father and mother. (1 Nephi 17:55.)

Despite their difficulties, the group finally arrived on the shores of a great sea and, under Nephi's direction, built a ship. They boarded the ship in order according to age, taking their wives and children with them, and set sail. After being driven before the wind for "many days," Laman and Lemuel, the sons of Ishmael, and their wives began to make merry, speaking with rudeness and forgetting God. Nephi worried that their actions would stop the Liahona from functioning and imperil the journey. So he spoke sharply to them. They responded by seizing and binding him. For four· days the winds blew against them, frightening the others on board and bringing Lehi and Sariah to their sickbeds, where they grew progressively more ill until Nephi felt sure they were about to die of their sorrows and be cast into a watery grave. He mentions how Jacob and Joseph, being young and in need of their mother's nourishment, suffered because of Sariah's sickness. Again Nephi's wife with tears and prayers rescued her husband, persuading Laman and Lemuel when "nothing but the power of God . . . could soften their hearts." (1 Nephi 18:20.)

A remarkable woman, twice she saved her husband's life, and she must have stood by Nephi while he was having trouble obtaining food for the camp and being blamed, even by his father, for his broken bow. At least she is not mentioned as a complainer. It cannot be by accident that Nephi follows the announcement of his marriage with the phrase, "I, Nephi, had been blessed of the Lord exceedingly." (1 Nephi 16:8.)

The Blessing of the Daughters of Laman and Lemuel

Sometime after Lehi and his party arrived in America, Lehi gave the daughters of Laman and Lemuel a final father's blessing. He told them if they heeded the commandments of God they would prosper in the land. He noted that children brought up in the way they should go do not depart from it, and he promised that if these children became cursed because of the traditions of their fathers, the curse would be taken from them and put upon the heads of their parents. He promised them that they would not perish, that the Lord would be merciful to their seed forever.

These blessings can be read as a grandfather's last tender pleading for the children he knows are not being reared in righteousness. Thus, they provide touching insight into Lehi and his loving concern for his family. But the blessings are also interesting because they were given to Laman's and Lemuel's daughters as well as their sons. The Bible, a much larger record, almost never records blessings given to daughters or even mentions that such blessings were pronounced. But Book of Mormon writers often acknowledge the influence of women on their descendants, praying that their influence will be righteous, as evidenced by the blessings Lehi gave his granddaughters. The generations of these children reach even to our day, and presumably they are still heir to those promises. Lehi gave the same advice and blessings to the sons of Ishmael and their "households," meaning the women of those households. (2 Nephi 4:3-11.) Unfortunately, these Ishmaelite women who sided with Laman and Lemuel are briefly mentioned in Alma (Alma 3:7) as believing the false traditions of their fathers, fulfilling the worst of Lehi's fears.

Nephi's Sisters

After Lehi's death, God warned Nephi to flee into a new wilderness. Again Laman and Lemuel were determined to kill him rather than be subject to their younger brother. Leaving, Nephi took his family; Zoram and his family (Ishmael's eldest daughter); Sam and his family; Jacob, Joseph, and his sisters. (2 Nephi 5:6.) This the only specific mention of "sisters" found in the Book of Mormon. That Nephi mentions "sisters" in the plural means that at least two went with him. He does not refer to these sisters as the wives of Ishmael's sons. And those married sisters, who had rebelled from the time they first came out of Jerusalem, would probably not have left their husbands to go with Nephi without his mentioning the fact. More likely, the sisters who accompanied Nephi were younger, born in the wilderness. That the birth of girls is not mentioned agrees with the custom of that day. Joseph is called Lehi's "last-born . . . in the wilderness," but "first-born" and "last-born" usually referred only to sons. More to the point, Nephi describes all who went with him as believers in the warnings and revelations of God. That speaks highly of his younger sisters.

Besides referring to the women who traveled with him, Nephi often mentions women representationally. Some of these references may not seem flattering, but they do allow us to draw useful analogies. In 1 Nephi, for example, the great and abominable church is repeatedly likened to a harlot and dubbed the "whore of all the earth." In the latter part of 2 Nephi 13, Nephi quotes Isaiah, using vivid descriptions of erring women rulers and haughty daughters of Zion in outlandish dress who "shall be desolate." But references of this kind are not numerous.

More often Nephi comments on the women of his family. But even these references are not frequent or full. Of the nine or more women who left Jerusalem with Lehi, only Sariah is mentioned by name. Often she and the other women in the wilderness are described with only snatches of action, but enough is given to show that they participated in every aspect of the wilderness journey. They pled, mourned, suffered, praised, prayed, complained, bore children, feared, and showed faith. Lehi sent his sons back twice, once for scriptures and once for wives, and Nephi found the strength of the women a prime matter for which to give thanks. Together these women became the mothers of the Nephite and Lamanite nations and emerge from the narrative as remarkably vital and individual.

More important, they round out the story of Lehi's exodus, helping us to keep a truer perspective on how the Lord works to accomplish his purposes. Think of it in this way: Noah took his family into the ark; Jared and his brother led their families from the tower; Moses brought families out of Egypt. Later, in the Book of Mormon, the northward migration from Zarahemla of 5,400 men included their wives and children, and Hagoth's vessels sailed with women and children aboard. (Alma 63:4-7.) Joseph Smith and Brigham Young paid particular attention to families in organizing the moves from Ohio to Missouri to Illinois and finally west in their modern-day exodus. (See D&C 51:3; 83; 90:28.) In every case, in every exodus or trek undertaken at the Lord's command or with his help, the women contributed significantly. Indeed the women and children were often the reason for undertaking such journeys, a fact the Book of Mormon writers are careful not to overlook.

The Women of Zeniff's Followers

Not only does the Book of Mormon acknowledge the importance of families in bringing to pass the purposes of God, but its writers suggest in both sermon and story that men ought to be responsible in their attitudes and actions toward women—and vice versa. This theme is not unique to the Book of Mormon. Moses counseled husbands against doing anything that might turn their wives' love from them, and he extended legal rights even to bondswomen. (See Deuteronomy 21:11-14.) He warned his people not to afflict or take advantage of the widow, stating that the nation that failed to care for its widows would come under condemnation and the sword of its enemies. (See Exodus 22:22-24.) At the same time, he made it clear that an adulterous daughter brought shame not only to herself but to her father. (See Leviticus 21:9.) And by assembling all Israel, male and female, bond and free, young and old, for the reading of the law, Moses placed everyone under the same obligations. These teachings would have been familiar to the Nephites.

But the Bible rarely returns to that theme. For example, much later the prophet Malachi warned husbands against dealing treacherously with the wife of their youth (Malachi 1:15), and the Apostle Peter warned that the husband who did not honor his wife would have his prayers hindered. (1 Peter 3:7.)

By contrast, the Book of Mormon returns to the theme more often. Nephi's brother Jacob recorded the Lord's delight in the proper treatment of women in one of the strongest statements on the subject in scripture: "I, the Lord, have seen the sorrow, and heard the mourning of the daughters of my people in the land of Jerusalem, yea, and in all the lands of my people, because of the wickedness and abominations of their husbands. And I will not suffer, saith the Lord of Hosts, that the cries of the fair daughters of this people . . . shall come up unto me against the men of my people. . . . For they shall not lead away captive the daughters of my people because of their tenderness, save I shall visit them with a sore curse even unto destruction." (Jacob 2:31-33.)

Clearly the Book of Mormon writers considered an appropriate attitude from husbands, fathers, brothers, kings, and priesthood holders more than a mere nicety. They saw it affecting the tenor of their nation's way of life and the blessings they would be entitled to receive. Nowhere is this better illustrated than in the story of the people who left Zarahemla with Zeniff, including the story of the twenty-four kidnapped daughters of the Lamanites.

After Nephi fled into the wilderness with his younger brothers and sisters, they settled in an area that came to be known as the land of Lehi-Nephi. Several generations later, the majority of the Nephites having become wicked and ripe for destruction, a man named Mosiah took as many righteous people as would follow him and fled this land. Mosiah and his people wandered northward until they discovered the land of Zarahemla, which was inhabited by the Mulekites, another people from Jerusalem who had come to America about the same time as Lehi and his family. These two groups united and chose Mosiah as their king. Nevertheless, Lehi-Nephi continued to be considered the homeland of the Nephites, and "a large number" wanted to return "to possess the land of their first inheritance." (Omni 1:27.)

An expedition was sent to study the possibility of a Nephite army taking the land of Lehi-Nephi by force, but dissension broke out. The leader of the expedition and some of the troops wanted to destroy the Lamanites. A man named Zeniff and some others, seeing "that which was good" among the Lamanites, were "desirous that they should not be destroyed," (Mosiah 9:1) but that a treaty be negotiated. The dissension became armed rebellion, and the expedition members fought among themselves until all but fifty were killed. Then Zeniff led the survivors back to Zarahemla, where they related what had happened to their wives and children.

This is the first mention of the wives and children of Zeniff's followers, who would become pivotal in the history of his people. The main narrative through this section of the Book of Mormon concerns battles and intrigues, the prophecies of Abinadi, and his final confrontation with King Noah.

Nevertheless, the women and children are mentioned over and over, building a repetitive pattern that emphasizes, amid the ebb and flow, how the fortunes of the nation hinged on the way the families were treated.

After relating his first unsuccessful venture into the land of Lehi-Nephi, Zeniff gathered a group of people who wished to possess the land and again journeyed into the wilderness. The trip was difficult, but eventually he and his followers arrived. They negotiated a treaty with the king of the Lamanites and took possession of Lehi-Nephi and the land of Shilom, where they immediately rebuilt cities, repaired walls, and planted crops. In particular, Zeniff credits the industry of the women, noting that they did "spin, and toil, and work all manner of fine linen . . . that we might clothe our nakedness; and thus we did prosper in the land." (Mosiah 10:5.) He acknowledges that such domestic skill added to the economic well-being of his people. Later when a Lamanite army came against him, Zeniff took time to hide the women and children in the wilderness before arranging the ranks of his soldiers, and he successfully drove the Lamanites back.

Unfortunately, Zeniff's son, King Noah, chose not to give women similar respect. The scriptures describe him as a man who followed "after the desires of his own heart," saying that he not only committed "whoredoms and all manner of wickedness," but that he "did cause his people to commit sin." In particular, he is said to have taxed his people one-fifth of all they possessed to support himself and his wives and concubines, his priests and their wives and concubines, and the harlots he and his priests liked to visit. When a Lamanite army came against him, King Noah commanded his people to flee together, but when the Lamanites began to overtake them, the king commanded his men to leave their wives and children and save themselves. That command divided King Noah's army. Some of his men preferred to perish with their families rather than leave them. The rest, including the king's priests, abandoned the women and children and fled with King Noah.

The Young Daughters Who Saved Their Families

Those who stayed behind with their families turned to their young daughters for help. Placing themselves in grave danger, these young women stood between the Lamanite army and their people and pleaded for the lives of their families. The scriptures do not record what these young women said, but they were successful. They moved the Lamanites to compassion, "for they were charmed" with their words and their beauty. (Mosiah 19:13-14.)

The Lamanites spared the lives of the women and children and the men who stood with them. These were allowed to return to their homes in Lehi-Nephi, but they had to agree to pay onerous yearly tribute to the king of the Lamanites. Having no other choice, they accepted the terms.

Among those men who stayed with the women and children was Limhi, King Noah's son. He was made titular king over his people on the condition that King Noah be handed over to the Lamanites. Limhi was aware of the iniquities of his father, yet he did not want to see him killed. So Gideon, a soldier who had long been opposed to King Noah, went secretly into the wilderness to search for the old king. There he encountered the main part of the king's men returning. They had reconsidered their loyalty to King Noah and sworn in their hearts that they would return to the land of Lehi-Nephi; if their wives and children were slain, they would seek revenge and die with them rather than live in the wilderness never knowing what had happened to their loved ones. When King Noah had become angry at their decision, they had turned on him and put him to death by fire, fulfilling Abinadi's prophecy.(See Mosiah 17:18.) They would have killed the king's priests as well, but the priests had escaped farther into the wilderness. Gideon told these men how their wives and children had been saved by their young daughters. They rejoiced and returned with their families to live under the Lamanite treaty. (Mosiah 19:19-24.)

The Twenty-Four Kidnapped Daughters
of the Lamanites

By contrast, the priests of King Noah further endangered their abandoned wives and children. Afraid to return to Lehi-Nephi, afraid the people would kill them if they did, these priests dared not reclaim their families; so having discovered a place near Shemlon where the daughters of the Lamanites met to sing and dance, they hid and watched them. One day when only a few of these young women had gathered to enjoy themselves, the priests of King Noah kidnapped twenty-four of them. (Mosiah 20:3-5.)

The Lamanites, angered at the loss of their daughters and supposing that Limhi and his people had perpetrated the deed, sent their army to destroy the inhabitants of Lehi-Nephi. King Limhi, seeing the Lamanite preparations for war, gathered his people together. They hid in the fields and forests and were able to surprise the Lamanite army and thus gain the advantage, though they were badly outnumbered— "not half so numerous as the Lamanites." The scriptures further explain their advantage by saying that they fought for their lives and "for their wives and for their children." (Mosiah 20:11.) These sentiments would come to be echoed almost word for word by Moroni in an equally desperate situation in which he would tear his coat and write on it, "In memory of our God, our religion, and freedom, and our peace, our wives, and our children," and raise it as a banner to rally his troops (Alma 46:12), and by numerous other leaders throughout Nephite history. (See 3 Nephi 2:12; Mormon 2:23; Ether 14:2.) The valor of Limhi and his people is described in poetic phrases: "they fought like lions for their prey," "like dragons did they fight." (Mosiah 20:11.) In the end they not only turned back the army, but they captured the king of the Lamanites, who was among the wounded the army left behind in its haste to retreat.

The people of Limhi cared for the Lamanite king's wounds, and when he had recovered, they brought him before King Limhi, wanting to slay him. King Limhi asked why he had come against them when Limhi's people had kept the treaty.

The Lamanite king explained about the twenty-four daughters who had been kidnapped and dragged into the wilderness. Limhi knew nothing of them, but he vowed to search among his people for the culprits. Gideon, the king's captain, immediately suspected the priests of King Noah, and he encouraged Limhi not to waste time searching among his own people but to tell the king of the Lamanites about these priests so that he and his people might be pacified. The Lamanites were already preparing for another battle—a battle the Nephites could not win, even by stratagem; they were so few and the Lamanites so numerous. Gideon added a note of poignancy to his plea, saying, "Let us put a stop to the shedding of so much blood."

King Limhi did as Gideon suggested. Then, unarmed, Limhi and his people went out to meet the Lamanites. The king of the Lamanites threw himself down before his own army and persuaded his people to turn back. Thus peace was restored, though at the price of further bondage.

Yet the people of Lehi-Nephi were not content to continue in such misery. They pleaded with King Limhi to go against the Lamanites to try to win relief. Three times they went to battle, and three times they were defeated. Widows mourned their husbands, and daughters mourned their fathers. The account says that only when there were many more women than men, and no hope of throwing off their oppressors, did the people of Lehi-Nephi remember to call on God. And even then God was slow to hear them because of their wickedness during the reign of King Noah. In their severely reduced circumstances, King Limhi commanded every man to contribute substance to the widows and their children that they might not perish—not an easy request considering that annually the Lamanites took half of everything they produced and that the priests of Noah had also begun to prey on them, sneaking into the land at night to steal grain and other supplies.

Hoping to reduce the plunder from King Noah's priests, King Limhi posted guards around the land. He wanted to catch the profligates who had abandoned their wives, stolen the daughters of the Lamanites, and caused such great misery among his people. Instead, Ammon and his brethren (who had come from Zarahemla seeking information about the people who had left with Zeniff) were mistaken for the priests, captured, bound, and brought before King Limhi. By this time, nearly all the prophecies of Abinadi had been fulfilled. The people of Lehi-Nephi had been "smitten on every hand and . . . driven." With the arrival of Ammon, the people knew that their prayers were once again being heard. Ammon taught King Limhi, who "entered into a covenant with God, and also many of his people." (Mosiah 21:32.) Knowing there was a land where his brethren were alive and well, King Limhi entertained the possibility that they might escape the oppression of the Lamanites and follow Ammon back to Zarahemla, but he would not consider any plan unless it included taking the women and children. That presented a problem, for with so many widows and orphaned children slowing them down, a Lamanite army would have no trouble overtaking them.

Gideon is credited with being "an instrument in the hands of God in delivering the people of Limhi out of bondage" (Alma 1:8), but the account does not elaborate on how he accomplished the deed. It says only that after getting the guards at the gate drunk, the people of Lehi-Nephi put their trust in God and departed into the wilderness, going around the land of Shilom. Then they joined Mosiah's people and became his subjects. Thus the women and children, including the many widows and orphans of the people of Lehi-Nephi, finally escaped the troubles that had come on them as a result of their iniquities and not believing the words of Abinadi.

Ironically, it was the Lamanite army pursuing Limhi and his people that finally discovered the priests of King Noah. Their wives, the twenty-four daughters of the Lamanites, seeing the army, went out and pleaded with their brothers

not to destroy their husbands. (Mosiah 23:30-34.) The Lamanites had compassion on these women and let their families live. More than that, Amulon, who was the leader of
the priests, was allowed to join the army of the Lamanites;
and while traveling through the wilderness, still searching
for Limhi, Amulon and the Lamanite army discovered yet
another group of Nephites, the followers of Alma.

Alma Escapes with His
Women and Children Followers

Alma had been a priest to King Noah, but he had been
converted by Abinadi and had left the king's service, taking
four hundred and fifty righteous souls with him, including
wives and families, and had gone into the wilderness. (Mosiah 23:1.) As with Limhi, Alma's followers would not consider leaving their families behind. They placed their trust
in the Lord, and they were strengthened, allowing them to
flee for eight days. Their flight was so fast that the army of
King Noah, marching without children and baggage, was
unable to overtake them. Once free of King Noah, Alma's
followers settled in "a land of pure water" and began building
a city they called Helam. There they lived in peace and prosperity, enjoying the fruits of their labors, until Amulon and
the Lamanite army discovered them.

Knowing they were outnumbered, Alma and his brethren
comforted their families, assuring them that the Lord would
"deliver them . . . that the Lord would soften the hearts of
the Lamanites." Then they delivered themselves unarmed
to the Lamanites, pleading for the sake of their wives and
their children, and the Lamanites spared them. By this time,
the Lamanite army was lost and promised that if Alma would
show them the way back to Lehi-Nephi, they would give
him and his people not only their lives but their liberty as
well. Alma showed them the way back, but the Lamanites,
now influenced by Amulon, failed to keep their part of the
bargain. Instead, they placed guards over the land of Helam

while part of the army returned to Lehi-Nephi to get the wives and children of the guards, indicating they intended to maintain an occupation force. Even worse, the king of the Lamanites placed Amulon over the people of Alma in the land of Helam. Thus Alma and his people found themselves in bondage to the same wicked priests they had fled from when Noah was king. Amulon, knowing that Alma had formerly been a priest like himself, took special pleasure in making the lives of Alma and his followers miserable. In particular, he tried to incite hatred between his children (the children of the twenty-four kidnapped daughters of the Lamanites) and the children of Alma. (Mosiah 24:8.)

But the Lord did not forget Alma and his people. Their burdens were eased, "made light," and their capacity to bear their bondage increased. Unlike Limhi's people, who had chafed under servitude, Alma and his followers submitted "cheerfully," with patience, until the Lord's voice came to them, saying: "On the morrow I will deliver you." (Mosiah 24:15-16.)

That night, Alma and his people gathered their flocks and their grain. The next morning when a deep sleep came on their persecutors, they took their families and fled, traveling all day. At evening they pitched their tents and lifted their voices in thanks. The scriptures say specifically that all the men and all the women and all the children who could speak praised God. (Mosiah 24:21-22.) Then they hastened on to Zarahemla.

Considering the effort Amulon made to engender hatred between his children and Alma's, it is interesting that among those who escaped to Zarahemla were some of the children of the twenty-four daughters of the Lamanites. Though their mothers had remained with the men who had forcibly abducted them, had even pleaded for their husband's lives, they had obviously never given their respect to Amulon and his fellow priests, and their children grew up hating their fathers.

When these descendants of the priests of Noah and the daughters of the Lamanites arrived in Zarahemla, they expressed displeasure with the conduct of their fathers, and they took the name of Nephi "that they might be called the children of Nephi" and be numbered among the Nephites. (Mosiah 25:12.) They were accepted by the people of Zarahemla — the scriptures say that "all of the people of Zarahemla were numbered with the Nephites." (Alma 25:4-9.)

Though nothing is said of any particular young woman among the twenty-four kidnapped daughters of the Lamanites, as a group they stand out. Remember that Zeniff, when he first reconnoitered the land of Lehi-Nephi, reported seeing much that was good among the Lamanites. Perhaps he had seen young women like those later captured by the wicked priests of Noah. These were women of moral strength despite the traditions of their fathers and despite the abuse they had suffered from their husbands. For whatever desires they had had as young girls, singing and dancing near Shemlon, their dreams were dashed the day they were torn from their families, abducted into the wilderness, and forced to become the wives of King Noah's priests. Yet they defended their families from the Lamanite army, even though their husbands were unworthy, and one has to believe it was their motherly influence that freed a part of their children. The teachings that the kidnapped Lamanite women passed on to their children eventually outweighed the violence and abuse of their fathers, and their children chose to become "Nephites."

Likewise, the women of Lehi-Nephi were courageous. It was their young daughters who saved their families from the Lamanite army. Though these women are mentioned repeatedly, they, too, are never distinguished individually. They are not even numbered. Nevertheless, their courage, welfare, and moral example are pivotal to the whole narrative — a fact emphasized by the way the Book of Mormon writers return to these women like a refrain, reaching back to the purpose behind the history.

Lamoni's Queen and Abish

Nowhere is the pivotal power of a single righteous woman better expressed than in the story of Abish, a Lamanite servant in King Lamoni's household. Yet her story is often overlooked in favor of the story of Ammon and his missionary brothers. But it seems likely that Ammon and his brothers would have had nothing to tell were it not for Abish.

Ammon is known as the great missionary of the Book of Mormon, and rightfully so. He and his three brothers labored fourteen years among the Lamanites, suffering "every privation" so that they might carry the gospel to their brethren, and they were successful. Their converts, thousands in number, took Ammon's name, calling themselves "the people of Ammon," and they were so grateful for the forgiveness of their sins that they chose death rather than take up arms and risk sinning again. (See Alma 24:5-16.) But initially Ammon and his brothers were not successful or even well received. In fact, they were all thrown in prison. Their success, nearly every success they had, can be traced directly to the royal household of King Lamoni, which had been carefully and patiently prepared by a servingwoman named Abish and by a queen who was willing to believe these missionaries in the face of what appeared to be the death of her husband.

Ammon and the other three sons of Mosiah renounced their father's throne to preach the gospel to the Lamanites, a plan that caused their fellow Nephites to laugh scornfully (Alma 26:23), for the Lamanites were "a wild and a hardened and a ferocious people." (Alma 17:14.) Nevertheless, they were determined and started their journey across the wilderness with fasting and prayer. In the wilderness they became discouraged and nearly gave up, but the Lord comforted them and said, "Go amongst thy brethren, the Lamanites, and bear with patience thine afflictions, and I will give unto you success." (Alma 26:27.) The Lord could make that promise, knowing that through Abish he had already prepared the way.

The scriptures describe Abish as a Lamanite woman who had been "converted unto the Lord for many years, on account of a remarkable vision of her father." (Alma 19:16.) The scripture is unclear about whether she had a vision in which she saw her father or whether her father had had a vision she accepted as truth. What matters is not how Abish came to know the Lord, but that she knew him; and she had maintained her faith in him quietly, steadfastly, while patiently waiting for a time to make it known to her people.

Ammon separated from his brothers, choosing the land of Ishmael for his labors. He was immediately captured, bound, and brought before King Lamoni. Lamoni asked Ammon if he wished to live in the land of the Lamanites. Ammon replied that he desired to dwell among the Lamanites for a time, perhaps even until he died, and Lamoni was sufficiently impressed to offer Ammon his daughter for a wife. Ammon had already refused one throne and had no wish to become connected to another. He told King Lamoni that he preferred to be his servant, so he was sent out to care for the king's flocks.

While being offered the hand of the king's daughter may have introduced Ammon to the women in Lamoni's household, it was not to be his last encounter with them. After saving the king's flocks with remarkable strength, Ammon was summoned before Lamoni and given an opportunity to explain by what power he was able to so serve the King. This was the opportunity Ammon had been waiting for. With the king's full attention, he started at the creation of the world and the fall of Adam and Eve and told the king the true traditions of his fathers and of God's love for all people. The king believed. His conversion was so complete that he fell to the earth breathing the prayer, "O Lord, have mercy."

The servants, thinking the king was dead, carried him to his wife. He lay on his bed as if dead for two days, his wife and sons and daughters mourning him. After someone had been dead two days, it was the custom among the Lamanites to place the person in a sepulcher; but Lamoni's queen was unsure of her husband's true condition and summoned Ammon instead.

He came asking what he could do for her. She addressed him forthrightly and without guile, telling him that the servants (undoubtedly including Abish) had told her that Ammon was a prophet who could do mighty works in God's name. Then she explained her present quandary about her husband, saying, "They say that he is dead and that he stinketh . . . but as for myself, to me he doth not stink." (Alma 19:5.)

Ammon knew that the king was not dead but under the power of God, and that the dark veil of unbelief was being cast from his mind. The queen had indicated some perception of what was going on, so after visiting the king's bedside, Ammon assured her that the next day—the third day—her husband would rise again. Then he asked, "Believest thou this?" Her answer was ingenuous. "I have had no witness save thy word and the word of our servants; nevertheless I believe." (Alma 19:9.)

The spiritual dimensions of Lamoni's queen must have been far greater than the few words used to tell her story, for Ammon blessed her and went on to say, "Woman, there has not been such great faith among all the people of the Nephites." This was extremely high praise, to be matched only by the first words her husband uttered after he awoke. Lamoni's queen watched over her husband from that time until the next day, when Ammon had promised the king would arise again. At the appointed time, he arose and stretched out his hand to his wife, saying, "Blessed be the name of God, and blessed art thou," praising the Lord and his queen in the same breath, confirming Ammon's high opinion of her.

He then went on to bear testimony directly to her. "I have seen my Redeemer; and he shall come forth and be born of a woman, and he shall redeem all mankind who believe on his name." In all, King Lamoni seemed to know two important facts about the Savior: that he would redeem those who believed in him, and that he would be born of a woman — a fact he seemed particularly anxious to share with his wife. When he finished telling her, he was filled with such joy that he was overcome again and sank into unconsciousness. The queen, too, was overcome by the Spirit and fell down. Ammon, seeing the great spiritual conversion being wrought by God, began to pour out his soul in prayer and thanksgiving until he too was overcome and sank to the earth. The servants, out of fear, also began to pray until they fell to the earth overcome — all except for one — Abish.

After years of waiting, now was her time to act. Recognizing that the power of God was working in the king's household, she saw her chance to convert her people. She hoped that if they beheld what was happening, they would believe. She ran from house to house gathering the people to come see the miracle.

Imagine her disappointment. When they came, they saw the king, the queen, and the servants all lying as if dead with Ammon, a Nephite; and they believed not in God but in their old superstitions and traditions, namely that a great evil had come upon the king and his household because he had allowed a Nephite to remain in the land.

A debate arose, and one man drew his sword to kill Ammon; but as he lifted his weapon, he was struck dead. The people marveled, not daring to touch any who had fallen. Some thought Ammon was the Great Spirit; others thought he was a monster sent by the Nephites to torment them. This contention continued until Abish became so frustrated and sorrowful at their lack of belief that she was moved to tears. Her great missionary effort having gone awry, she stepped forward and took the queen by the hand. Immediately the queen stood and cried with a loud voice: "O blessed Jesus, who has saved me from an awful hell! O blessed God, have mercy on this people!" (Alma 19:29.)

Lamoni's queen clasped Abish's hand and, filled with joy, spoke in tongues, saying many things not understood by the others in the room. Then she raised King Lamoni, who immediately began preaching to the people, who were still arguing over what they were seeing. Unfortunately, many of them would not hear the king's words and went their own way.

When Ammon arose, he administered to the observers that remained, and all the servants awoke declaring the same things—that their hearts had been changed; that they had no more desire to do evil. They said they had seen angels and conversed with them; that the angels had told them the things of God and of his righteousness. Some of those Abish had gathered believed and were baptized and became a righteous people—the beginning of the Church among the Lamanites.

Abish's great joy in these events is shown by the fact that she "ran forth from house to house making it known." She who had been prepared years before by her belief in a miraculous vision, who had waited faithfully for the moment when she would be able to declare her belief, was at last witnessing the spiritual awakening of her people. Perhaps restrained from declaring herself openly, she nevertheless had worked quietly among her associates. Twice her queen had declared that she was willing to believe Ammon because of the word of her servants, one of whom was Abish. How had Abish cultivated her Queen's trust? How had she nurtured her own faith, secretly living her religion while waiting for the moment when she could reveal it? And when Ammon prayed until he was spiritually overcome, did he give thanks for the faith and foresight of Abish? The story is too brief, leaving many questions unanswered; but faith like the queen's, "greater than any among the Nephites," does not blossom overnight. The household of King Lamoni had been carefully cultivated by Abish the servingwoman.

Lamoni's Father's Queen Was Unprepared
for the Miracle She Saw

The observers Abish had gathered lacked the same spiritual
preparation. She had had no time to prepare them as she
had prepared King Lamoni's household, and they had no
way to account for what they were seeing but to blame Ammon, a Nephite, in the tradition of their fathers. Similarly
unprepared, another queen, the wife of Lamoni's father, an-
grily commanded that Ammon's brothers be killed when she
saw her husband spiritually overcome.

Lamoni, wanting to bring Ammon before his father,
wished to journey with him to the land of Nephi, but Ammon
was told by the Lord to go to Middoni instead because his
brothers were in prison there. Lamoni believed in the word
of the Lord and went with Ammon to Middoni. On the way,
they met Lamoni's father, who was king over all the Lamanites.

Lamoni's father, angry at Lamoni for harboring a Nephite,
tried to kill his own son, but Ammon withstood him and
gained the advantage. He made the king swear in exchange
for his life not to harm Lamoni and to free Ammon's brothers.
When Lamoni's father saw that Ammon did not wish to harm
him and that his son truly loved this Nephite, he became
interested in what Ammon had to say. He wanted to learn
the words Ammon had taught his son.

After freeing Ammon's brothers, Ammon and Lamoni
returned to the land of Ishmael and established a church
there, with King Lamoni allowing his people freedom of
worship. Meanwhile, Ammon's brothers traveled to the land
of Nephi to Lamoni's father's house and offered to be his
servants. When he asked about Ammon, whom he had desired to hear, they explained that the Spirit of the Lord had
prompted him to go another way and teach the people of

Lamoni. Lamoni's father was troubled by this and asked Aaron and the rest of Ammon's brothers to explain the workings of the Spirit. Aaron explained the gospel, beginning with the Creation and telling him of the Christ who would atone for the sins of the world. The king believed. He offered to forsake his kingdom and all he possessed to receive the joy of redemption. Aaron suggested that he bow down and call on God. He did, crying out, "O God, Aaron hath told me that there is a God . . . and I will give away all my sins to know thee." (Alma 22:18.) When he had said this, he was struck as if he were dead, just as his son Lamoni had been.

As with Lamoni, the servants of this king ran to the queen. When she saw her husband lying as if dead, she commanded her servants to slay the missionaries. But the servants had seen the cause of the king's fall and dared not lay hands on them. They pleaded with the queen not to make them do this thing until, seeing their fear, the queen also began to be afraid. She sent her servants to gather the people, hoping that when they saw what had happened, they would kill Aaron and his brothers.

Aaron, seeing the determination of the queen and knowing the hardness of the people, feared that such a group would only create more contention, so he put forth his hand and commanded the king to stand, and he stood. This made the queen and her servants marvel and fear. The scriptures say that the king ministered to them until his whole household, presumably including the queen, were converted. (See Alma 22:19-24.)

When the people, who had gathered at the queen's command, began to murmur, the king stood among them and administered to them. When the crowd was quiet, he had Aaron and his brothers preach. This was the beginning of Aaron's success among the Lamanites. Eventually he and his brothers converted many souls to Christ, but they lacked the help of a faithful servingwoman like Abish. In the end, their results were never as spectacular as what had transpired in King Lamoni's household.

Amalickiah's Queen Was Concerned for Her People

One other Lamanite queen is mentioned in the Book of Mormon. Her husband was killed by Amalickiah, a conspiring Nephite who wished to be king over the Lamanites and had already murdered his way to the head of the Lamanite armies. He sent an emissary to the queen, informing her of her husband's death and blaming it on the former king's servants.

To her credit, the queen's first concern was for her people. She pleaded with Amalickiah to spare the people of the city and not bring his army against them. (Alma 47:32-33.) Then she requested that he bring witnesses to testify about the death of the king. Amalickiah took the same servants he had hired to slay the king and all who were involved with him in the plot. They testified that the king had been killed by his own servants, citing as evidence the fact that the servants had run away. In fact, the servants had fled when they realized Amalickiah meant to blame them for the king's death. In this way Amalickiah satisfied the queen about her husband's death.

This queen must have been powerful in her own right, or Amalickiah, who was high-handed in everything else he did, would not have taken such pains to placate her about her husband's death. He went on to seek her favor and eventually married her, thus consolidating his hold on the Lamanite kingdom. Later Amalickiah was killed by one of Moroni's generals. His brother, who succeeded him as king, sent news to the queen that she was again a widow. The fact that his brother would immediately send such a communication while in the middle of a battle again suggests that this woman was a powerful queen, one that even armies paused to give respect.

More Lamanite Women Are Singled Out in the Book of Mormon than Nephite Women

The Book of Mormon, according to its introductory paragraphs, was "written to the Lamanites. . . . " For that reason, it may be significant that more Lamanite women are singled out in this scripture than Nephite women. Almost without exception they are worthy, courageous women who dared look beyond the traditions of their fathers to embrace truth — perhaps in fulfillment of the specific blessing Lehi gave the daughters of Laman and Lemuel. (See 2 Nephi 4:3-9.)

Among those singled out are Lamoni's father's queen, who was converted with her household; Amalickiah's queen, who expressed concern for her people above her own feelings; and the twenty-four kidnapped daughters of the Lamanites. But the two Lamanite women most singled out by the text are Lamoni's queen and Abish — Abish being one of only three new-world women mentioned by name in the entire Book of Mormon. The others are Sariah, the wife of Lehi; and Isabel, a harlot named in the book of Alma.

Lamoni's queen exercised faith sufficient to sustain her in the face of what appeared to be the death of her husband; sufficient to gain Ammon's praise and her husband's acknowledgment; sufficient to speak in tongues and raise her husband the second time he was spiritually overcome. Likewise Abish, the servant who already knew of Christ before Ammon arrived, proved herself particularly well practiced in the use of her faith. Not only had she learned of Christ through a vision, but she had sustained her belief in that vision over the years, incorporating Christian attributes into her life. She made herself the epitome of the "good servant," a theme the Savior would use over and over in his teachings about himself and his followers. When it came time for her to acknowledge her beliefs, her example had already spoken so eloquently there was little else to add.

The Mothers of the Stripling Warriors

Instilling faith in the next generation has remained the ultimate challenge of parents since the time of Eve. Eve had walked with God and talked with the tempter; but having fallen, she found herself limited as all mothers are limited — she could not force that knowledge on her children. She could not even love that knowledge into them. She could only testify, exemplify, teach, preach, and pray, and then hope her children would be moved by their own spiritual stirrings to seek the truth for themselves. Yet, despite that limitation, faithful mothers have succeeded with their children more often than not. Throughout the scriptures a consistent pattern emerges of righteous mothers rearing righteous children. But of all the worthy mothers in scripture, one group stands out — the Ammonite mothers of Helaman's two thousand stripling warriors.

Their story begins with their own commitment to live the gospel. After Ammon had converted King Lamoni's household with the help of Abish, Ammon and his brothers took the gospel message to other parts of the Lamanite kingdom, eventually converting Lamoni's father. When Lamoni's father died, his son, Lamoni's brother, took the name of the converted Lamanites — "Anti-Nephi-Lehi" — as his own name and ascended the throne. Immediately those Lamanites who had not been converted rebelled against the new king and took up arms. Concerned for the welfare of their new converts, Ammon and his brothers traveled to the land of Ishmael to counsel with King Lamoni and his brother, King Anti-Nephi-Lehi, to decide how they should defend themselves.

In that moment of crisis, King Anti-Nephi-Lehi addressed his people. He thanked God for having been granted the chance to repent. Of his people he said, "We were the most lost of all mankind. . . . It was all we could do to repent sufficiently." Then he expressed his fear that such repentance might not be possible a second time, saying "If we should stain our swords again they can no more be washed bright." (Alma 24:12-13.)

The occasion was a war council, yet the king boldly proposed that his people not take up arms — that they die, if need be, before harming one of their brothers. He asked them to bury their swords and other weapons as a testimony to God that it was better to die than commit sin.

Among those who heard King Anti-Nephi-Lehi were the women who would become the mothers of the two thousand stripling warriors. With the rest of their people facing an enemy army, they pledged their lives.

When the other Lamanites, their unconverted brethren, came against them, intent on destroying the king and placing one of their own on the throne, the people of Anti-Nephi-Lehi prostrated themselves on the ground in prayer. The enemy killed a thousand and five converts before they realized the people of Anti-Nephi-Lehi would not flee nor turn aside but die praising God. Moved by their courage and conviction, many of the opposing army were converted—more than had been slain.

The attitude of the people of Anti-Nephi-Lehi is revealed in the reasoning they gave for their actions. Those who perished were righteous and assured salvation, but because they had refused to shed the blood of their unconverted brothers, no wicked person perished in that battle to suffer eternal consequences.

The women who would be the mothers of the stripling warriors witnessed those events. They incorporated those understandings into their experience.

Sacrificing self rather than shedding blood was not something the people of Anti-Nephi-Lehi did once in a fever of faith. When their enemies came against them a second time, they again allowed themselves to be killed rather than risk killing one of their brothers. Following this second battle, Ammon could no longer tolerate seeing his converts massacred. Knowing that they would never have peace in their own land, he suggested they flee to the land of Zarahemla.

Among those making that journey were the mothers of the young warriors. Some may have carried in their arms babies who would grow up to be among the warriors. Others likely gave birth in the wilderness to sons who would also be numbered in the ranks of the two thousand.

The people of Zarahemla accepted the converts of Ammon and his brothers, and gave them the land of Jershon. They agreed to set their armies around Jershon to protect the people of Anti-Nephi-Lehi, asking only that they give of their substance to help maintain those armies. (Alma 27:21-24.)

The women who were to be the mothers of the two thousand stripling warriors knew of God's promise to preserve them and, seeing that promise fulfilled, they incorporated that into the catalog of experiences they would pass on to their sons and their daughters. These women and the rest of Ammon's people are described as being "perfectly honest and upright in all things; and they were firm in the faith. . . . Thus they were a zealous and beloved people, a highly favored people of the Lord." (Alma 27:27-30)

Following that description, the scriptures do not say much about these mothers and the other people of Ammon during the years when they reared their sons, except to note that they took in another group of exiles who were driven out of the land of Zorom because of their beliefs. (Alma 35:6-9.) But the scriptures do make it clear that those were not easy times in which to rear a righteous generation.

All was not well in Zarahemla. Alma, the chief priest over the land, found himself struggling with some of his own sons. Korihor, the antichrist, won many followers away from the church. Isabel, a harlot in the land of Siron, "did steal away the hearts of many." (Alma 39:3-4, 11.) At the same time, the Lamanites attacked the Nephite borders. Yet through all that, undaunted, the mothers of the young warriors quietly cultivated the faith of their sons and daughters.

The pressure from the Lamanites increased. They repeatedly battered at the Nephite borders until several cities were lost. Internal strife also increased, threatening to topple the Nephite judges. As things worsened, the people of Ammon saw the danger and felt "moved with compassion" because of the tribulations the Nephites and their armies had borne for them. Seeing how beleaguered they were, fighting against the Lamanites on so many fronts, the people of Ammon considered setting aside their vows and taking up arms—not in their own defense, but in defense of those who had so generously defended them for so many years.

Helaman, a son of the prophet Alma and one of the "high priests over the church," argued against their breaking their vows. Like King Anti-Nephi-Lehi, he "feared lest by doing so they should lose their souls." (Alma 53:15.) Before being converted, the people of Ammon had been steeped in the bloodthirsty traditions of the Lamanites and were in danger of slipping back into those traditions if they took up arms again, even in a good cause. Helaman eloquently persuaded them to honor their sacred covenant, even though the Nephites were in danger.

But by this time the people of Ammon had children who had been born after the people had made their vow. These children were not bound by that vow, so two thousand of the sons of the Ammonites, still young, entered into a new covenant. They covenanted never to give up liberty but to fight to protect the Nephites and themselves from bondage, and they asked Helaman to be their commander. (Alma 53:16-19.)

At this point, Helaman pauses in the scriptural narrative to explain that defending the people of Ammon had never been a disadvantage to the Nephites, but a source of many blessings. (Alma 53:19.) God had commanded the Nephites "to defend themselves, and their families, and their lands, their country, and their rights, and their religion." (Alma 43:46-47.) But the people of Ammon, with a different background, had made a different covenant with the same God. Helaman acknowledges that God can direct different people different ways in the same situation depending on his purposes. Helaman also acknowledges that the Ammonites had contributed generously to the support of the Nephite armies and adds that now they also became a great support because of their sons.

Those sons of the Ammonites made up an unlikely army. They were inexperienced young men reared by parents whose pacifism was their most sacred commitment. Helaman may have had doubts about their fighting ability, but he never doubted their character. He describes them as "exceedingly valiant . . . men who were true at all times in whatsoever thing they were entrusted" — words remarkably similar to those used to describe their mothers years earlier.

In a letter, Helaman tells Moroni how he marched the two thousand warriors to Judea to assist Antipus, the appointed leader of the southern campaign. He praises God that seeing the addition of his two thousand soldiers, the Lamanites held off for a time, allowing the Nephites to strengthen their defenses. The Nephites then continued at a stalemate with the Lamanites. The Ammonite fathers of the two thousand warriors brought generous provisions. Another two thousand men from Zarahemla also arrived, bringing provisions for themselves and their wives and children. (Alma 56:28.) The Lamanites, seeing the Nephites' increasing numbers and supplies, grew restless and began ambushing anyone carrying provisions. Seeing that, Helaman and Antipus devised a strategy.

Helaman marched his army of young warriors toward a neighboring city as if carrying provisions. On their way, they marched near the city of Antiparah, which housed the largest and strongest Lamanite army. As Helaman and Antipus had suspected they would, the Lamanite army gave pursuit. Helaman's young soldiers marched straight northward, leading the most powerful army of the Lamanites away from the protection of Antiparah. Then Antipus took his army, leaving only a small number to defend their city, and went after the Lamanite army.

When the Lamanites realized they were being pursued by Antipus, they did not turn and fight as Helaman and Antipus had expected. Instead, they marched straight for Helaman's young warriors, probably thinking to slay them before Antipus could overtake them and thus lessen the danger of being surrounded in the open. Antipus, realizing the danger to Helaman's young untested troops, sped his army, hoping to overtake the Lamanites. But night overtook all three armies, and they made camp.

At dawn the Lamanites still pursued Helaman and his troops. Helaman, thinking his young soldiers were no match for the mightiest Lamanite army, advanced northward, marching as hard as he could into the wilderness, not daring to turn right or left for fear of being overtaken. They fled in this manner all day.

At dawn the next day, the Lamanites still pursued; but on the third day, Helaman realized the Lamanites were no longer after them. That left him in a quandary. He knew they were no longer being pursued, but he did not know whether Antipus had overtaken the Lamanites or whether the Lamanites lay in wait to ambush him and his troops the moment they turned.

Helaman explained the situation to his young soldiers and asked, "Will ye go against them to battle?" Their response astounded and deeply moved him. He wrote to Moroni: "Never had I seen so great courage, nay, not amongst all the Nephites." The young men Helaman called his sons told him they wanted to go to battle, fearing that unless they did, the Lamanites would overpower Antipus and his troops. They explained that they had no desire to kill their brothers if they would leave them alone, but they had sworn to defend their liberty and the liberty of the Nephites. They did not fear, for they had been taught by their mothers "that if they did not doubt, God would deliver them." Helaman says that they rehearsed to him the words of their mothers, saying, "We do not doubt our mothers knew it." (Alma 56:46-48.)

Helaman turned and marched his army back. Antipus had overtaken the Lamanites, and a terrible battle was in progress. Weary from having marched so far so fast, Antipus' army was being slaughtered. Antipus himself had fallen by the sword with many of his leaders. If Helaman and his "sons" had not come to their aid, all would have been lost. Helaman's young soldiers engaged the battle, and suddenly the whole Lamanite army turned on them.

After the battle, Helaman numbered the young men. He feared that, being inexperienced, many of them had died. To his joy, he found that not one had fallen, though they had fought with such ferocity that they had frightened the Lamanites into becoming prisoners.

Sixty more young Ammonites came to join Helaman's troops. In a later battle, the Lamanite army descended on Helaman and would have overpowered him except that his little band of two thousand and sixty soldiers fought desperately and remained firm before the Lamanites when his other troops would have given way.

Helaman writes that they obeyed every command with exactness and were blessed according to their faith. He adds that in that moment of crisis, he found his own inspiration: "I did remember the words which they said unto me that their mothers had taught them."

Following the battle, Helaman again counted his losses. Two hundred of his two thousand and sixty young men had fainted for loss of blood, and none of his young "sons" had escaped without receiving "many wounds." But not one had perished. Their preservation was astonishing to Helaman's whole army, for more than a thousand other soldiers had died in the battle. He adds, "We do justly ascribe it to the miraculous power of God, because of their exceeding faith in that which they had been taught to believe" by their mothers. (Alma 57:25-26.)

Helaman mentions his young troops one more time, saying that they were with him in the city of Manti. He repeats that not one of them had been slain though all had received many wounds. Then he goes on to praise their strict obedience to God's statutes and their continual faith in the words of their mothers.

Following the battles in which their sons stood firm in faith and deed, the people of Ammon and the Nephites of Zarahemla prospered and enjoyed years of peace. Helaman, the son of Helaman, describes those years, emphasizing the free trade between the two peoples and their fine craftsmanship in precious metals. He mentions growing grain and raising flocks. He also praises the women, noting especially that they made fine-twined linen. (Helaman 6:13.) But unquestionably the finest accomplishment of those women was the rearing of a righteous generation — sons firm in faith and daughters and granddaughters who were "exceedingly fair." (3 Nephi 2:16.)

Does a mother's righteousness assure her sons' safety in war? No. The Ammonite mothers of Helaman's stripling warriors enjoyed a special blessing based on their faith and the faith of their sons. Yet questions remain. How did these mothers succeed amidst turmoil and dissension when even the prophet Alma struggled spiritually with some of his sons, having to take time away from the affairs of the church to exhort them to repentance? In what ways did those mothers support each other to make their success collective? What exactly were the words that the young men rehearsed to Helaman that so astounded and inspired him?

The specifics of how the Ammonite mothers instilled such faith into their sons are not fully known, but Jesus, when he visited the Nephites, named the power by which these women taught their children. He said: "Whoso cometh unto me with a broken heart and a contrite spirit, him will I baptize with fire and with the Holy Ghost, even as the Lamanites, because of their faith in me at the time of their conversion were baptized with fire and with the Holy Ghost, and they knew it not." (3 Nephi 9:20.)

The Maidservant of Morianton

One other woman mentioned specifically in the Book of Mormon affected the outcome of a battle. Morianton's maidservant was the victim of abusive violence. Not willing to let herself be victimized, she changed the circumstances of her own life and, in the process, greatly affected the lives of many Nephites, ensuring their freedom as well as her own. Her story begins with a land dispute in the twenty-fourth year of the Nephite judges.

The land of Morianton and the land of Lehi lay next to each other, both near the north sea, east of Zarahemla. The people of Morianton, led by a man also called Morianton, claimed part of the land of Lehi and armed themselves, determined to press their claim by the sword. The people of Lehi, who were in the right about the disputed territory, appealed to Moroni and his army to come to their aid. Morianton, not wanting to confront Moroni's army, decided to take his people and flee in the opposite direction, northward toward Bountiful, and seize control of "the land covered with large bodies of water."

Had Morianton succeeded, particularly in winning over the people of Bountiful to his cause, which greatly concerned Moroni, the consequences would have been serious, possibly leading to the overthrow of the Nephite government. At the least, it would have placed a hostile army at the rear of Moroni's forces, cutting them off in the north at the narrow neck of land. Morianton was a brilliant tactician, and the scriptures state that he would have succeeded were it not for his maidservant. (See Alma 50:30-32.)

Morianton may have been a genius at military strategy, but he had no self-control. "Being a man of much passion," he became angry with one of his maidservants and beat her severely. She fled to Moroni's camp and told him of Morianton's plans.

Moroni sent an army that stopped Morianton at the borders of the land of Desolation. A battle ensued in which Morianton was slain and his army defeated. The people of Morianton were brought back, and, after covenanting to keep the peace, they were restored to their own land. The people of Lehi also returned to their own land.

Morianton's maidservant may or may not have perceived the larger ramifications of her actions. But whatever her motive, it was firmly rooted in a sense of her own self-worth.

She was not willing to submit to personal violence and took the most direct and effective action available to her.

Women have often been the objects of violence, especially in times of armed conflict. As victims of atrocities, prisoners of war, and bereaved refugees, the women of the Book of Mormon suffered through years of fighting, paying again and again the high price of war. They were not immune to torture and death by the sword, nor to rape and abuse. Mormon wrote in a letter to his son Moroni, "The suffering of our women and our children upon all the face of this land doth exceed everything." (Moroni 9:19.)

Strife both within and without the Nephite nation increased until battles, with their accompanying death and destruction, became almost commonplace. In the Book of Mormon, the slain are regularly numbered, and battle strategies are outlined in detail. By contrast, the women are mentioned infrequently and then usually in a context suggesting that their need for protection inspired the Nephite soldiers to stand their ground and persist longer in the face of overwhelming Lamanite numbers, the implication being that the Nephite soldiers were fighting for the "more just cause." But actually these women for whom the soldiers were fighting may have been closer to the battlefront than one might initially suppose.

Helaman, noting the addition of two thousand new troops to his army, mentions their wives and children and that the soldiers had brought provisions enough for themselves and their families, indicating that when the soldiers moved from post to post, they took their families with them. That placed families on the front line (Alma 56:28) and explains the inequity Moroni faced when he negotiated with Ammoron for an exchange of prisoners. The Lamanites were holding many Nephite families captive, while the Nephites had only Lamanite warriors. Moroni threatened to arm his women if Ammoron did not agree to exchange one Nephite family for every Lamanite warrior. (Alma 54:12.) Later he actually smuggled arms into the prisoners being held by the

Lamanites in the city of Gid, "even to their women, and all those of their children, as many as were able to use a weapon of war." (Alma 55:17.)

On another occasion Alma and Amulek saw the women and children of Ammonihah brought together and questioned by unbelievers. Those who believed in the word of God were burned along with their records and holy scriptures. (Alma 14:8-10.) When Amulek saw the suffering of these women and children, he wanted to save them by the power of God. Alma stopped him, saying, "The Spirit constraineth me . . . for the Lord receiveth them up unto himself." (Alma 14:11.) He explained that God did not intervene every time the wicked inflicted suffering on the innocent, so that the wicked might be judged for what they had done. The women and children of Ammonihah, despite their painful exit from mortality, were received into heaven as heirs of the kingdom. Their tormentors faced an eternity of torture among the damned. Alma and Amulek escaped to the land of Sidom. There they found other refugees from Ammonihah and related to them "all that had happened unto their wives and children." (Alma 15:2.)

As the Nephite nation faced its final destruction, the depravity with which women were treated by both sides became indistinguishable. The Lamanites took men, women, and children prisoners from the tower of Sherrizah. Then they killed the men and fed them to their wives and children. (Moroni 9:7-8.) On the other side, the Nephites took prisoner the daughters of the Lamanites, and, after raping them, tortured them to death and then ate their flesh as a sign of bravery. (Moroni 9:9-10.)

How did the women caught in those dire circumstances cope? According to the scriptures, some turned inward for strength. Following one tremendous battle that left hundreds of Nephite women widowed with children to rear, they mourned and fasted and prayed. (Alma 28:5-6.) Others, like Morianton's maidservant, seized the opportunity and changed the course of events.

Jesus Among the Nephite Women

After the tempests, earthquakes, fires, and whirlwinds that followed the Savior's crucifixion, darkness covered the land of the Nephites and Lamanites. In that darkness the people mourned because of the great destruction that had befallen them, and because they had not repented earlier. If they had repented, they said, "then would our mothers and our fair daughters and our children have been spared." (3 Nephi 8:25.)

Out of the darkness came a voice — not a harsh voice, nor a loud voice, but a piercing voice — that echoed those same sentiments, saying: "Wo, wo, wo unto this people because of the slain of the fair sons and daughters." (3 Nephi 9:2.)

Jesus addressed the men and women of the Nephite nation out of the darkness. He enumerated the great destructions that had befallen the Nephites because of their wickedness, and he pleaded with the righteous remnant to come to him. He asked for their broken hearts and contrite spirits. He promised that if they would make such an offering, he would baptize them with fire and the Holy Ghost. He then gave them an example they knew. He explained that he had baptized the mothers of the stripling warriors with fire and the Holy Ghost many years previously. (3 Nephi 9:20.)

When the people heard the voice again, after several hours of silence, Jesus spoke of himself as a mother hen who wanted to gather her chicks under her wings to protect and nourish them, but whose children would not come. He repeated that thought, using that motherly image several times, and then was silent again.

Later when the Savior appeared in person to the Nephites, he literally gathered the little ones to him like a mother hen, and he blessed them and showed great miracles through them. In Israel, Jesus had acknowledged the Jewish mothers who had sought his blessing for their children, saying, "Suffer the little children to come unto me, and forbid them not; for of such is the kingdom of God." (Mark 10:14.) Among the Nephites, he did not wait for the women to approach him with a request. He commanded that the little ones be brought to him. The scriptures describe the scene, saying that the multitude parted so that the children might come forward. When the children were all gathered around him, Jesus asked the multitude to kneel. Then he knelt himself. Surrounded by the Nephite children, Jesus prayed, and the scriptures say that "the things which he prayed cannot be written. . . . The eye hath never seen, neither hath the ear heard, before, so great and marvelous things as . . . Jesus [spoke] unto the father." (3 Nephi 17:11-17.)

The multitude was overcome with joy. Jesus arose, wept, and blessed them for their faith. He took the children one by one and blessed them and prayed to the Father for them. When he had finished, he wept again.

Then, turning to the multitude, Jesus said, "Behold, your little ones." The multitude saw the heavens open. Angels descended and encircled the children as if with fire, ministering to them. According to Nephi, an apostle who was writing the record, the multitude numbered two thousand five hundred souls, men, women, and children. All saw and all bore record.

On a later visit to the Nephites, Jesus loosened the tongues of the children, and the scriptures tell of how they spoke great and marvelous things. Even the babes opened their mouths and uttered things so wonderful that Nephi was forbidden to record them. (3 Nephi 26:14, 16.) Jesus explained that he was showing greater things to the Nephites than anything he had shown the Jews because their faith was greater, and he admonished the Nephites to "pray in your families unto the Father, always in my name, that your wives and your children may be blessed." (3 Nephi 18:21.) The scriptures add that following these marvelous manifestations, "every man did take his wife and his children and did return to his own home." (3 Nephi 19:1.)

The people of the Book of Mormon had looked forward to the coming of the Savior and had been given signs by which they might know when that time was near. They had also honored his mother for many years. Nephi saw her in a vision shortly after his father first left Jerusalem. He saw how she was carried away in the Spirit to conceive, and when he looked again, he saw her with the babe in her arms. King Benjamin, when he spoke to his people for the last time, also told of the woman who would be the mother of the Savior and declared that her name would be Mary. Alma likewise told the people of Gideon about Mary, calling her "a virgin, a precious and chosen vessel." (Alma 7:10.) When Ammon preached to King Lamoni, the king was overcome with the Spirit and fell to the earth as if dead. He lay unconscious for three days. When he regained his consciousness, one thing that he was particularly anxious to tell his wife was that he had seen the great woman who would be the mother of the Savior.

After all that had been prophesied of Jesus, his birth, and his atoning sacrifice, the righteous Nephites were most anxious for his coming. Those who actually saw him considered being a witness a great privilege. Feeling his wounds and witnessing his miracles was an event the prophets themselves had hoped to see. Yet the small evidences sometimes strike the most resonant chord. No doubt one way the Nephite women recognized their Savior was from how he included them in his teachings, blessing the children and talking of "mother hens," an image to which they could relate. Even when speaking through his servants the prophets, the Savior had always included women in his teachings.

The people of King Benjamin's time covenanted to become "children of Christ, his sons, and his daughters." (Mosiah 5:7.) The Lord told Alma the Younger not to marvel that men and women of all nations must be born again to be "redeemed of God, becoming his sons and daughters." (Mosiah 27:25.) And Nephi had invited both sexes to "come unto [the Lord] . . . male and female . . . [for] all are alike unto him." (2 Nephi 26:33.) With similar language Amulek promised that the resurrection "shall come to all . . . both male and female" and that men and women will "be arraigned before the bar of Christ the Son of God . . . to be judged according to their works." (Alma 11:44.)

The Savior had addressed the Jaredites, saying: "I am Jesus Christ. In me shall all mankind have life . . . and they shall become my sons and my daughters." (Ether 3:14.) And he touched the stones that the brother of Jared had brought him and caused them to shine that they might give light to the men, women, and children. (Ether 6:3.)

In an incident that foreshadowed Jesus' calling the little children to him, Alma had blessed the women and children of the city of Gideon (Alma 7:27) and the women and children in Amulek's household (Alma 10:11). He acknowledged that God "imparteth his word by angels unto men, yea, not only men but women also. Now this is not all; little children do have words given unto them many times which confound the wise and learned." (Alma 32:23.)

The humble recognize their Savior, whether they be young or old, bond or free, male or female; and the Nephite women and their families were no exception. They knew their Lord because they had heard his voice before, speaking through his servants — speaking directly to them.

The Daughter of Jared and Other Jaredite Women

As all scripture testifies of Jesus, the Book of Mormon is a witness to Christ. That is its primary purpose. It is also a history of Christ's dealings with more than one nation. Although mainly about the Nephites, the Book of Mormon also tells of a separate, earlier people called the Jaredites who were destroyed by their wickedness just before the Nephites arrived to take their place. As Nephite women had a great influence on their nation, so did the Jaredite women.

The Jaredites knew the strength of their daughters. Jared and his brother listed their daughters in their genealogies. The scriptures are full of lengthy rosters of fathers and sons, but, as a rule, daughters are mentioned only intermittently and then usually only when special circumstances require it. That the Jaredites included their daughters, even briefly, makes them unusual, especially given the number of daughters listed in such a short record.

Included by the Jaredite writers are references to Jared's daughters; the friends and brother of Jared's daughters; Orihah's eight daughters; Corihor's daughters; Shule's daughters, some of whom were born to him in his old age; and Omer's daughters, who were divinely protected when their enemies conspired to destroy them and their father. The list continues with Emer's daughters; Coriantum's daughters, begotten in his old age; Heth's daughters; Shez's daughters; Kim's daughters, who were born and lived in captivity with their father while he was the prisoner of his brother who had usurped the throne; Levi's daughters; Corom's daughters; and Lib's daughters. Near the end of the record, the daughters of Coriantumr, Cohor, and Corihor are said to be unrepentant like their fathers, and they contributed to the overthrow of the Jaredite nation. Most of these women are mentioned briefly and only as daughters; but one, the daughter of Jared, is discussed at greater length. And, remarkably, the fall of the Jaredites can be traced directly to this ambitious young woman.

At the Tower of Babel, Jared, his brother, and their families received a promise from God that their language would not be confounded, and that they would be led to a choice land. Under the Lord's direction, they journeyed a great distance, built barges, and crossed the ocean. Once established on the American continent, they settled down to till the soil and rear families. They grew in prosperity because of the blessings of the Lord.

These people, who called themselves Jaredites, had many kings, some righteous, some not. Prophets traveled the land crying repentance, and when the kings protected these prophets, allowing them free travel and free speech, the people repented and the land prospered in peace.

Then a man named Jared, a descendant of the first Jared, rebelled against his father, the king, and took control of the kingdom. His father, Omer, spent most of his days in captivity, where many of his younger sons and daughters were born. Then two of Omer's younger sons raised an army and fought Jared. They defeated Jared's army and would have killed him had he not pleaded for his life, saying he would give the kingdom back to his father if they would spare him. And so Omer became king once again. Jared was then out of power and became despondent, "for he had set his heart upon the kingdom and upon the glory of the world." (Ether 8:7.) It was into these circumstances that the daughter of Jared stepped forward with such fateful consequences.

She is described as a capable woman, "exceedingly expert" and "exceedingly fair" (Ether 8:8-9), meaning intelligent and beautiful. Seeing her father grieve, she decided to help him win back the kingdom. She had read the ancient records of the creation of the world and the history of mankind — records the Jaredites had brought with them from the Tower of Babel. These records contained not only an account of God's dealings with his children, his promises and his commandments, but also a record of the secret oaths and covenants with the devil (3 Nephi 6:28) by which men and women had obtained kingdoms and great worldly glory in the past. These secret combinations had been known since the time of Cain, who had entered into such a covenant with Satan, calling himself "Master Mahan" and glorying in his wickedness. (See Moses 5:29-33.)

The daughter of Jared went to her father, reminded him of those secret combinations, and suggested that they avail themselves of the power of Satan. She urged her father to send for Akish, the son of Kimnor, who was the king's friend. The daughter of Jared boasted of her beauty and said, "I am fair, and will dance for him, and I will please him, that he will desire me." She suggested that the price for her hand in marriage should be the head of King Omer.

Events transpired exactly as the daughter of Jared planned. Akish became so fascinated with her that he was willing to consider killing the king to win her hand. But first Akish gathered the household of Jared, including Jared's daughter, and made them swear to be faithful to him in the heinous deed he was about to perform. They swore by the God of heaven, the heavens, the earth, and their own heads, vowing that anyone who refused to help Akish or divulged anything of their secret organization would die. Then Akish administered the "oaths which were given by them of old who also sought power, which had been handed down even from Cain. . . . And they were kept up by the power of the devil . . . to help such as sought power to gain power, and to murder, and to plunder, and to lie, and to commit all manner of wickedness and whoredoms." (Ether 8:15-16.)

The scriptures state plainly that Jared's daughter persuaded her father to search up these old oaths. Jared persuaded Akish, and Akish administered it to his kindred and friends, promising them whatever they desired. "And [together] . . . they formed a secret combination, even as they of old; which combination is most abominable and wicked above all, in the sight of God." (Ether 8:18.)

By the use of these secret combinations, Akish and his followers contrived to overthrow the kingdom of Omer. But the Lord, who allows the wicked the freedom to seek their own destruction, never allows his own purposes to be thwarted. He warned King Omer of their intentions in a dream, and Omer took his family and fled for many days. At last, coming to a place called Ablom, which was by the ocean, he and all his household but Jared and his family pitched their tents and dwelt there in peace.

Meanwhile, Omer being gone, Jared was appointed king, and he gave Akish his daughter to be his wife. But the wickedness that the daughter of Jared had unleashed spread faster than she could control it. Akish murdered Jared, now his father-in-law, as he sat on his throne giving audience, and Akish reigned instead. In time Akish became jealous of his own son (presumably also the daughter of Jared's son) and had him imprisoned and starved to death. (Ether 9:5-7.)

Another son, Nimrah, was angry with his father for what he had done to his brother. Gathering followers, he escaped and went to live with Omer, his great-grandfather. Akish and the daughter of Jared had other sons who had sworn allegiance to their father and to do iniquity as he desired, but they offered the people money to follow them instead of their father. Because the people were as corrupt and greedy as their king, they followed his sons. The sons of Akish warred against him for many years until nearly the whole nation was destroyed. Only thirty people survived. They fled and joined Omer, who was then restored to the throne.

After she married Akish, the daughter of Jared is never mentioned again. Whether she died in the battles between her husband and her sons or lived to see the destruction of the Jaredite kingdom remains untold. Akish killed the father she had been willing to engage the forces of hell to help, and he starved her son in prison. Had she become so wicked as to be emotionally untouched by those actions? Or did she live to bemoan the betrayal caused by the forces she herself had put into motion?

Of the kings that followed, some were righteous and some were not, but all had to deal with the secret combinations that the daughter of Jared had unleashed. Emer was righteous enough to see Jesus Christ in a vision, and his son Coriantum followed in his father's footsteps and was greatly blessed, with one exception: he had no children. Despite that disappointment, like Abraham of the Old Testament he honored his wife and remained faithful to her until, being one hundred and two years old, she died. Then he married a young maid and had sons and daughters by her, living to be one hundred and forty years old. By contrast, a later king named Riplakish took many wives and concubines, the costly support of which caused his people to rebel. They killed him and drove his descendants out of the land. King Com fought the robbers who had adopted the ancient evil oaths, but he did not prevail against them. One of his sons rebelled and put the prophets to death. As a result, such a great calamity came on the people that the bones of those who died were heaped in piles, and there were wars and famines and pestilences. And still the wickedness introduced by the daughter of Jared continued.

The prophets withdrew because of the wickedness of the secret societies. The last prophet sent to the Jaredites was Ether. Though his prophecies were "great and marvelous," the people cast him out.

The daughters of Coriantumr, Cohor, and Corihor are mentioned as being among the "fair sons and daughters" who rejected Ether and refused to repent. (Ether 13:17.) Coriantumr, who was studied "in all the arts of war and all the cunning of the world," fought those who wanted to destroy him, and soon "all the people upon the face of the land were shedding blood, and there was none to restrain them." Women and children were killed, their bodies scattered across the land, their numbers mounting to more than two million dead. (Ether 14:17, 22.) In the end, they took up arms themselves, "both men, women and children being armed with weapons of war, having shields, and breastplates, and head-plates, and being clothed after the manner of war" (Ether 15:15), and they fought to the last man, woman, and child. The "fair" and unrepentant daughters of Coriantumr fought in that final battle. It was the last day of their lives and the lives of all the unrepentant women of the Jaredite nation.

One theme reiterated again and again in the Book of Mormon is the culpability of women who do not actively seek righteousness for themselves, their families, and their nation. Several verses lament the fate of destroyed daughters who might have been saved if they had repented sooner (3 Nephi 8:25; 9:2; Mormon 6:19; Ether 13:17). And, according to Jacob, those who fight "against Zion . . . both male and female, shall perish." (2 Nephi 10:16.) In the time of Alma, Korihor the antichrist led many women astray (Alma 30:18); and Isabel the harlot led many men astray (Alma 39:3-4). The consequences of sin redound whether it is actively advanced or passively accepted. Nowhere is that more evident than in the consequences suffered by the Jaredite women.

The daughter of Jared, a young woman "exceedingly fair" and "exceedingly expert," dared enter the devil's league. As a result, she introduced the secret organization to her people that led to their destruction. Others might have prevented that holocaust, but instead they dabbled in those same oaths and covenants and "spread works of darkness and abominations over all the face of the land, until he [the devil] dragged the people down to an entire destruction." (Helaman 6:28.) It happened to the Jaredites; it happened to the Nephites; and it can happen again.

Indeed, it is that sense of the overwhelming power to influence that pervades the Book of Mormon references to women and distinguishes them. Even when Book of Mormon writers include individuals such as Abish or the daughter of Jared, their stories seem not to stand alone so much as to reiterate that larger theme. Often with unforgettable imaginative power, the Book of Mormon illustrates with stories like that of the mothers of the stripling warriors how personal decisions affect not just the tenor of a particular home but the history of nations. Entire sections of this scripture meticulously develop that idea as the underpinnings of the surface narrative. To overlook the women of ancient America is to miss a main point.

Yet admittedly the references are brief, scattered, and easily underestimated. Even with close examination, most of the women remain nameless and in the background. Yet when these references are gathered and considered as a group, they yield surprising depth and dimension, and one comes to realize that often even the more dramatic elements of the history depend on the women.

Without the young daughter of Ishmael who pled for his life, Nephi would never have arrived in America; without Abish, Ammon and his brothers would never have converted the Lamanites; without Morianton's maidservant, Mormon would have lost the land northward; and without the faithful mothers of the stripling warriors, Helaman would have lost an army and likely a free nation. The writers of the Book of Mormon knew that, and though writing on metal plates was difficult and demanded brevity, they were careful to include the contributions of their sisters.

References

Sariah
1 Nephi 1:1; 2:5; 5:1-10; 8:2-16; 17:1-2, 20, 55; 18:6-7, 17-19; 2 Nephi 3:1

Wife of Ishmael
1 Nephi 7:6, 19

Daughters of Ishmael
1 Nephi 7:6, 19; 16:7, 19, 27, 31, 35-36; 17:1-2, 20; 18:6, 9, 19; Alma 3:7

Nephi's Wife
1 Nephi 7:19; 16:7, 35; 18:19

Eldest Daughter of Ishmael (Zoram's wife)
1 Nephi 7:6; 16:7, 35; 2 Nephi 5:6

Wives of Ishmael's sons (Lehi's daughters)
1 Nephi 7:6; 18:9; 2 Nephi 4:10

Daughters of Laman and Lemuel
2 Nephi 4:3-6, 8-9

Nephi's Sisters
2 Nephi 5:6

"Whore of all the earth" and other feminine images (largely drawn from Isaiah) used by Nephi in his account
1 Nephi 13:7-8, 17, 34; 14:9-13, 16-17; 21:1, 15, 18, 22-23; 22:6, 13-14; 2 Nephi 6:6-7; 7:1; 8:18, 25; 9:21, 36; 10:9, 16; 13:12, 16-24; 14:1, 4; 15:14; 19:1, 17; 20:2, 30, 32; 23:16; 24:2; 26:32-33; 28:18

The Twenty-four Kidnapped Daughters of the Lamanites
Mosiah 20; 21:20; 23:30-34; children of: Mosiah 25:12; Alma 25:4-9; 43:13

The Women and Children of Zeniff's Followers
Mosiah 11:2, 4, 14; 19:9-24; 21:9-10, 17; 22:2, 8

The Women and Children of Alma's People in the Land of Helam
Mosiah 18:34; 23:28; 24:22; Alma 2:25; 3:1; 7:27; 10:11

Concern for Wives and Children Theme in Book of Mormon
Jacob 2:7, 28-35; Mosiah 10:9; 21:17; 22:2, 8; 23:28; Alma 1:30; 2:25; 3:1-2; 7:27; 10:11; 15:2; 35:14; 43:9, 45; 44:5; 46:12; 48:10, 24; 53:7; 54:11-12; 56:28; 58:12, 30-31; 60:17; 63:4-6; 3 Nephi 2:12; 3:13; 8:25; 18:21; 19:1; Mormon 2:23; Ether 6:3; 14:2

Lamoni's Queen
Alma 18:43; 19:1-5, 8-30

Abish
Alma 19:16-29

Lamoni's Father's Queen
Alma 21:21; 22:19-24; 23:3

Amalickiah's Queen
Alma 47:32-35; 52:12

Lamoni's Daughter
Alma 17:24; 18:43

The Mothers of the Stripling Warriors
Alma 24 and 27 (background); 53:16-21; 56:3, 5-6, 9-10, 30-36, 45, 48, 55-56; 57:6, 19-27; 58:39-40; 3 Nephi 2:16 (daughters of Ammonite mothers mentioned); 3 Nephi 9:20 (power by which Ammonite mothers taught)

Isabel the harlot
Alma 39:3-4, 11

Maidservant of Morianton
Alma 50:30-31

Suffering of Book of Mormon Women
1 Nephi 16:35; Mosiah 21:9-10; Alma 2:25-26; 3:2; 14:8-11; 15:2; 28:5; 48:24; 53:7; 54:3; 58:30-31; 60:17; Helaman 11:33; 3 Nephi 8:23-25; Mormon 4:14-15, 21; 6:7; Moroni 9:7-10, 16, 19

Jesus Among the Nephite Women
3 Nephi 9:2, 18:21; (they worship him) 17:10, 25; 19:1; (calls little children to him) 17:10-11; 26:14-16 (see also) Matthew 19:13-15; Mark 10:13-16; Luke 18:15-17

Jesus as Mother Hen
3 Nephi 10:4-6; 22:1-8; 24:5; Luke 13:34; Isaiah 31:5; D&C 10:65

Mary, the Mother of Jesus (Book of Mormon References)
1 Nephi 11:13, 15, 18-20; Mosiah 3:8; Alma 7:10; 19:13

Genealogies of Jaredite Daughters
Ether 6:15, 16, 20; 7:2, 4, 12, 14, 26; 8:1, 4; 9:2-3, 21, 24, 25; 10:2, 14, 16, 17, 29; 13:17

The Daughter of Jared
Ether 8:8-17; 9:4-7

Coriantum's Wives
Ether 9:24-25

Coriantumr's Daughters
Ether 13:17, 15:2, 15, 23

2
Women in the Doctrine and Covenants

The current edition of the Doctrine and Covenants contains few references to women, and the references are all brief. One wonders why. The Doctrine and Covenants is *the* latter-day book of scripture—the one most addressed to the current time. In this dispensation when women's roles have been most questioned, wouldn't one expect to find more detail and clearer guidelines?

The answer lies in the character of the Doctrine and Covenants, which is made up of selected revelations received by Joseph Smith and other presidents of Christ's latter-day church—revelations that deal largely with the establishment and administration of that church: priesthood functions.

Other characteristics also make the Doctrine and Covenants unique among the books of scripture. For example, the Doctrine and Covenants is historical in that it is drawn from events in the modern history of the Church. But it does not relate those events chronologically as the Bible and the Book of Mormon relate the events of their time. If it did, it would undoubtedly have included stories on the contributions of pioneering women in the early days of the Restoration; but it doesn't. In fact, the Doctrine and Covenants contains almost no stories. When individuals are mentioned, their deeds are usually not; rather, the individuals are given specific direction on various subjects. Often other historical narratives must be used to discover why an individual received divine instructions and how well he or she followed the advice.

Given those overall characteristics, the references to women are understandably few, and yet we should not overlook the fact that those few are surprisingly significant. It is the Doctrine and Covenants that reveals a woman's potential—to become a goddess (D&C 132:20)—and her important responsibilities in the next world (D&C 138:39). No other scripture supplies that information as clearly.

With regards to women, the Doctrine and Covenants might be best described as echoing, illuminating, and expanding other scriptures. For example, three women are named in the Doctrine and Covenants: Emma Smith, Vienna Jaques, and Eve. But in every case, those references connect with other scriptures and historical sources to expand our understanding beyond the initial few words. The reference to Eve illustrates this most aptly.

Joseph F. Smith was pondering Christ's three-day visit to the spirit world following the Savior's death and before His resurrection. A vision, now recorded in section 138, opened, and President Smith saw the righteous dead assembled in paradise and Christ's ministry among them. He saw many prophets and also "our glorious Mother Eve, with many of her faithful daughters" engaged in the work there, teaching and laboring among the spirits. The reference connects to other references, adding an additional dimension to our understanding of Eve, "the mother of all living," and expands, like the vision it records, to offer today's sisters a glimpse of life beyond the veil—truly an eternal perspective.

Going beyond the obvious references, some concern for women can be inferred from the mention of families. When Thomas B. Marsh was called to preach the gospel, he was told to govern his house in meekness, and he was assured that his family would be blessed. (D&C 31:2, 5, 9.) Likewise Joseph Smith and Sidney Rigdon, who had been long absent from their homes, were assured that their families were well. (D&C 100.) Brigham Young was told that he would no longer have to leave his family to serve the Church as he had previously. (D&C 126.)

Also interesting are the numerous references in the Doctrine and Covenants to the parables Jesus taught women during his lifetime. Jesus took particular care to include in his teachings many stories that featured women as the main characters or that included experiences with which women were familiar, such as baking bread or birthing babies. The care with which Jesus taught women during his earthly ministry is inspiring, and the repeated references to those same parables scattered throughout the Doctrine and Covenants suggest that the stories of the virgins and their oil (Matthew 25:1-13; D&C 33:17; 45:65; 63:54), the hen and her chicks (Luke 13:34; Isaiah 31:5; D&C 10:65; 29:2; 43:24), and the widow and the unjust judge (Luke 18:2-5; D&C 101:81-84) may have particular significance for our modern era.

There are other brief specific references to women, but section 83 focuses entirely on a discussion of widows and orphans under the United Order. Because this section is short and the Church does not presently practice the United Order, it is easy to overlook. But the problems mentioned in section 83 connect with similar concerns expressed in the other scriptures, illustrating the consistency of the Standard Works—a testimony in itself.

Section 83 Illustrates God's Consistent Concern for His Widowed Daughters

Joseph Smith received the revelation in section 83 while visiting Jackson County, Missouri, in the spring of 1832. Traveling with Sidney Rigdon, Jesse Gause, and Newel K. Whitney, he came to Independence to help the local elders work out the practical problems of settling the members on land administered under the law of consecration. He and several of his associates were deciding problems of stewardship when a question came up about what to do when the bread-winner of a family died leaving a dependent wife and chil-dren. The Prophet describes events leading up to the reve-lation in these words: "On the 27th [of April 1832], we transacted considerable business for the salvation of the Saints, who were settling among a ferocious set of mobbers, like lambs among wolves. It was my endeavor to so organize the Church, that the brethren might eventually be inde-pendent of every incumbrance beneath the celestial kingdom, by bonds and covenants of mutual friendship, and mutual love.

"On the 28th and 29th, I visited the brethren above Big Blue river, in Kaw township, a few miles west of Independ-ence, and received a welcome only known by brethren and sisters united as one in the same faith, and by the same baptism, and supported by the same Lord. The Colesville branch, in particular, rejoiced as the ancient Saints did with Paul. It is good to rejoice with the people of God. On the 30th, I returned to Independence, and again sat in council with the brethren, and received the following: . . . " (Joseph Smith, *History of the Church of Jesus Christ of Latter-day Saints,* 7 vols., 2nd ed. rev., edited by B. H. Roberts [Salt Lake City: The Church of Jesus Christ of Latter-day Saints], 1:269.)He then wrote out the six verses of the revelation.

The Lord had given Joseph Smith previous command-ments concerning women. In June 1829, the Lord com-manded that all women be baptized. (D&C 18:42.) On Feb-ruary 9, 1831, he commanded men to love their wives, and he placed both men and women under the same obligation to confess or be brought to Church trial in cases of adultery. (D&C 42:22, 80-93.) Then, on January 25, 1832, the Lord spoke with his prophet at length on the duty of the Church to support the families of those who had been called to leave their homes to preach the gospel. (D&C 75:24.) In section 83, the Lord reminded Joseph of those previous revelations and then extended the Church's obligations to include widows and orphans.

The revelation states that women have claim on their husbands and fathers for their support. If the husband or father dies and the woman has remained faithful, then she has claim on the Church and the Lord's storehouse. If the woman is a transgressor, is unfaithful, or is affiliated with some other church, the property deeded to her husband as his stewardship is to be transmitted to her in accordance with the laws of the land. Having received her husband's property, she has no further claim on the Church. Such women were free to seek support from the laws of the land instead of being supported by the laws of stewardship under the United Order. (See D&C 51.)

Likewise the revelation decrees that children have claim on their parents, both mother and father, until they are of age, and it makes similar provisions for them as it does for women.

Joseph Smith did not simply admonish his followers to care for widows and orphans and then leave those followers at their own discretion as to how to carry out that Christian mandate. Under the Lord's direction, he sought to frame institutions by which Church members might literally become their brothers' and sisters' keepers. Interesting, and yet, as stated before, section 83 is short and obviously minor. What value does the student of the scriptures gain from attention to this section?

As with many of his revelations, in section 83 Joseph Smith restores more than he reveals. The revelation in section 83 connects with other scriptures to point out the consistent concerns for women that the Lord has expressed through his prophets in every age. That connecting, reaffirming aspect of the revelation gives it significance.

Like Joseph Smith, Peter and Paul
Were Concerned About Widows

In New Testament times, the Apostle Paul wrestled with a problem similar to that faced by Joseph Smith. (See 1 Timothy 5:3-11.) Like the Prophet, Paul was concerned with the practical application of Christian principles. The church in his day was in a crisis because the needs of the poor, specifically widows, were outstripping available funds. Under the direction of the Lord, Paul taught that children and grandchildren should care for their widowed mothers, saying that if they failed to provide for their own, they were worse than infidels, for even the pagans of that day recognized the need to care for their mothers.

About the same time Paul was instructing Timothy about the care of the widows in Ephesus, a dispute arose in Jerusalem that involved Peter and several of the other apostles. The Greek-speaking members of the Jerusalem branch of Christ's church, who were in the minority, had accused the Hebrew-speaking members of neglecting Greek widows, giving them less food and clothing than their Hebrew sisters. The Twelve summoned a meeting and called on the brethren to elect seven men to oversee the distribution of charity. (Acts 6:1-5.)

Like Joseph Smith, Old Testament Prophets
Provided Institutions to Care for Widows

In Old Testament times, the need to provide safeguards for widows was even greater, as widows inherited nothing from their dead husbands. Inheritance passed first to the sons, then to the daughters, then to the husband's brothers, then to the father's brothers, and so forth. (Numbers 27:8-11.) The widow was left to return to her father's house or depend on the charity of her sons or her husband's kinsmen. If she had no father and no sons, she often faced dire circumstances.

On several occasions, the Lord took personal responsibility for widows, saying that he would be their judge, and that he would relieve them. (Deuteronomy 10:18; Psalms 68:5; 146:9; Proverbs 15:25.) But more often the Lord provided specific laws and institutions to protect and provide for widows and orphans. Israel as a nation was commanded to provide for widows at their festivals and out of their offerings. They were to leave the gleanings of the fields and to give tithes of wine, corn, oil, and the firstlings of the flocks. (Deuteronomy 24:19-21.)

Book of Mormon Prophets Believed That the Welfare of Their Nation Hinged on How Well They Provided for Widows

Book of Mormon prophets frequently mentioned widows and warned their leaders not to neglect them. Prophet after prophet stated that the welfare of the Nephite nation hinged on how well the widows were treated. (See 2 Nephi 20:1-2; Mosiah 21:16-17; 3 Nephi 24:5.) Following the final destruction of his people, Moroni reiterated that theme in a poignant warning. He spoke of the day when his writing would come forth, and he warned the people of that day (us) not to "cause that widows should mourn." (Mormon 8:40.)

The concern that Joseph Smith and the brethren in Missouri showed by asking the Lord about widows and orphans fits into a long tradition of the Church, the prophets, and the Lord providing institutional safeguards for the welfare of single women. Such care identifies a righteous people.

On January 14, 1847, at Winter Quarters, Brigham Young, following in that long tradition, asked for instructions from the Lord about the care of the widows and orphans in the Mormons' forced exodus west. The Lord commanded that each company take an equal number of the poor, the widows, the orphans, and the families of those who had gone into the Mormon Battalion. He added the familiar warning to prophets of every age that these things needed to be done "that the cries of the widow and the fatherless come not up unto the ears of the Lord against this people." (D&C 136:8.)

Vienna Jaques, A Single Woman, Was Asked to Give Her Fortune to the Church

Considering the consistent concern the scriptures express for widows, it would not be surprising that the reference to Vienna Jaques in section 90 of the Doctrine and Covenants also concerns the participation of women in the United Order. In this case, Vienna Jaques was not a widow but a single woman who had never married. Also, through her own efforts, she had amassed a small fortune. She was addressed in the revelation as "my handmaid." In four verses, she was admonished to consecrate her money to the Church and to move to Zion (Missouri) that she might receive an inheritance from the bishop there and "settle down in peace . . . and not be idle in her days." Nothing else was said, leaving the reader to wonder: Did she follow the prophet's advice? Did she give her money to the Church? Did she go to Missouri? And since no Mormon who went to Missouri in that day "settled down in peace," how did she react when that part of the prophecy was seemingly not fulfilled?

The reference to Vienna Jaques is a good example of the need to include historical materials in a study of the Doctrine and Covenants. Without the reference's historical background, it is cryptic and of little value; but with its historical context, the advice given to Vienna Jaques takes on meaning and importance—not the least of which is how Vienna's whole life seemed to lead up to the moment she received divine communication and then pivoted on how she responded.

Vienna was born in New Rowley (now Georgetown), Massachusetts, on June 10, 1787, making her approximately the age of Joseph Smith's parents. She was the daughter of Henry and Lucinda Jaques. Her father was an immigrant from France, her mother a direct descendant of John Rogers, the English martyr. When Vienna came of age, she moved to Boston, and, according to her own description, with "self-reliance, patient toil and strict economy," probably working as a nurse, managed to accumulate more than $1,400, which was a considerable amount of money for the time.

She was a devout Christian and had associated with the Methodists, receiving "sanctification" as a member of the Bromfield Street church in Boston. But soon she became dissatisfied and began investigating several other Christian sects, seeking a church that evidenced the spiritual gifts described in the New Testament. Hearing of a new prophet in the West who had published a sacred record, she sent for the Book of Mormon and read it. At first she was unimpressed, but then late one evening as she walked home from a church meeting, she contemplated what the theme of her evening prayers should be. Suddenly she saw a vision of the Book of Mormon, and she resolved to ask about its truthfulness. Her conversion was not instantaneous but came gradually with continued study of the scriptures. As she tells it, after praying, she was able to more fully comprehend the book. She continued to read until her mind "was illuminated" and she became convinced of its divinity.

In 1831, traveling alone by canal and stagecoach, she made her way to Kirtland, Ohio. She described her journey to a reporter years later as "an arduous undertaking"; but she was "strong and concentrated in purpose, braving all danger and trusting in the Almighty for protection," and her way "was marvelously opened up."

In Kirtland, she met the Prophet and, after being further instructed, was baptized. She stayed in Ohio about six weeks and then returned to Boston, where she became the means of converting her mother, her sister, and her nieces, who were also baptized. They remained in the East, but Vienna was determined to join the Prophet and his other followers. She concluded her affairs in Boston, collected her valuables, and returned to Ohio, where, on March 8, 1833, she was instructed by revelation to give her money to the Church and settle in Missouri. (D&C 90:28-31.)

Vienna was in her mid-forties, past an age when most of her contemporaries would have considered giving up the security of a hard-earned nest egg to take up the uncertainties of life on the edge of the western frontier, especially as a lone woman. But she accepted the Prophet's advice and relinquished her wealth, turning it over to the Church. Joseph Smith acknowledged her contribution, giving her credit for having done a great service both to himself and to the Church; both he and the Church were nearly destitute at the time. In turn, Vienna received means from the Church (a portion of her own money returned to her) to help her make the journey to Missouri. She may have intended to leave immediately, but on April 30, 1833, at a Kirtland conference of high priests, it was decided that she should wait and travel with a company headed by William Hobart. On July 2, 1833, Joseph Smith mentioned her in a letter, commenting on how happy he was to have heard of her safe arrival.

Promised Peace, Vienna Jaques
Found None in Missouri

In Missouri, Vienna received the inheritance she had been promised, probably a parcel of land in Jackson County, from Bishop Edward Partridge. But she never realized any benefit from it. The Saints in Jackson County had already been harassed, and the persecutions intensified just as she arrived. She was probably driven from her land shortly after she received it, for she seems to have been among the displaced when Zion's Camp, led by Joseph Smith, arrived a year later.

Zion's Camp consisted of between one hundred and fifty and two hundred Kirtland brethren who had come to Missouri hoping to force Governor Dunklin to address the difficulties of the Saints. The camp arrived in Jackson County in the spring of 1834 and opened negotiations, asking the governor to use the state militia to help the Saints repossess the land they had been forced to leave. The governor admitted that their request was just, but he refused to order out the militia for fear of inflaming a civil war within his state. Disheartened by the failure to "redeem Zion" and other disappointments that had plagued Zion's Camp from the beginning, Joseph disbanded the organization on the 24th of June. On the eve of that disbandment, cholera broke out among the camp members with such violence that within four days thirteen were dead, not counting the Missouri Saints, some of whom also died.

Heber C. Kimball noted in his journal that about midnight he "began to hear the cries of those who were seized. . . . Even those on guard fell with their guns in their hands to the ground, and we had to exert ourselves considerably to attend to the sick, for they fell on every hand." He described the growing difficulty of facing "enemies without and the destroyer within." He told of standing guard while they dug graves and of his frustration and sorrow at seeing his brethren so severely stricken "who had traveled a thousand miles through so much fatigue." But then he added, "I received great kindness from . . . sister Vienna Jaques, who administered to my wants and also to my brethren—may the Lord reward . . . [her] kindness."

No detail is offered about how Vienna Jaques aided the members of Zion's Camp, but Heber C. Kimball's praise of her is almost the only positive note in his narrative of that summer's march, and it closely resembles Joseph Smith's praise in a letter he addressed to Vienna from Ohio after the Zion's Camp episode.

In this letter, which Vienna would prize for the rest of her life, Joseph offered an explanation about why things had not gone well for her in Missouri. Nothing suggests that she had asked for such an explanation. Quite the opposite, the Prophet noted that he had been prompted to write by the Spirit, and he stated that her prayers were the source of the prompting. He reassured her that her offering (the donation

of her money) was acceptable, "respected by the Lord," and
that notwithstanding her present difficulties, she would be
blessed. His letter, dated September 4, 1833, reads:

> Dear Sister: —Having a few leisure moments, I sit down
> to communicate to you a few words, which I know I am under
> obligation to improve to your satisfaction, if it should be a
> satisfaction for you to receive a few words from your unworthy
> brother in Christ. I received your letter some time since, con-
> taining a history of your journey and your safe arrival, for
> which I bless the Lord; I have often felt a whispering since I
> received your letter, like this: "Joseph, thou art indebted to
> thy God for the offering of thy Sister Vienna, which proved
> a savor of life as pertaining to thy pecuniary concerns. There-
> fore she should not be forgotten of thee, for the Lord hath
> done this, and thou shouldst remember her in all thy prayers
> and also by letter, for she oftentimes calleth on the Lord,
> saying, O Lord, inspire thy servant Joseph to communicate
> by letter some word to thine unworthy handmaiden, and say
> all my sins are forgiven, and art thou not content with the
> chastisement wherewith thou hast chastised thy hand-
> maiden?" Yea, sister, this seems to be the whispering of a
> spirit, and judge ye what spirit it is. I was aware when you
> left Kirtland that the Lord would chasten you, but I prayed
> fervently in the name of Jesus that you might live to receive
> your inheritance, agreeable to the commandment which was
> given concerning you. I am not at all astonished at what has
> happened to you, neither to what has happened to Zion, and
> I could tell all the whys and wherefores of all these calamities.
> But alas, it is in vain to warn and give precepts, for all men
> are naturally disposed to walk in their own paths as they are
> pointed out by their own fingers, and are not willing to con-
> sider and walk in the path which is pointed out by another,
> saying, This is the way, walk ye in it, although he should be
> an unerring director, and the Lord his God sent him. Never-
> theless I do not feel disposed to cast any reflections, but I feel
> to cry mightily unto the Lord that all things which have hap-
> pened may work together for good; yea, I feel to say, O Lord,
> let Zion be comforted, let her waste places be built up and
> established an hundred fold; let Thy Saints come unto Zion

out of every nation; let her be exalted to the third heavens, and let Thy judgment be sent forth unto victory; and after this great tribulation, let Thy blessing fall upon Thy people, and let Thy handmaid live till her soul shall be satisfied in beholding the glory of Zion; for notwithstanding her present affliction, she shall yet arise and put on her beautiful garments, and be the joy and glory of the whole earth. Therefore let your heart be comforted; live in strict obedience to the commandments of God, and walk humbly before Him and He will exalt thee in His own due time. I will assure you that the Lord has respect unto the offering you made. Brother David W. Patten has just returned from his tour to the east, and gives us great satisfaction as to his ministry. He has raised up a church of about eighty-three members in that part of the country where his friends live—in the state of New York. Many were healed through his instrumentality, several cripples were restored. As many as twelve that were afflicted came at a time from a distance to be healed; he and others administered in the name of Jesus, and they were made whole. Thus you see that the laborers in the Lord's vineyard are laboring with their might, while the day lasts, knowing "the night soon cometh when no man can work." (signed) Joseph Smith

Sometime in 1838, before the Saints were driven out of Missouri, Vienna Jaques married Daniel Shearer, a blacksmith and whipmaker from New York who had joined the Church in 1832 and come to Far West. He was a widower with grown children and was active in Church affairs in Missouri. Daniel Shearer and Vienna Jaques would seem to have been kindred spirits, active in the pursuit of their beliefs and deeply caring of those who were less fortunate. Shortly after their marriage, Daniel was jailed for having helped rescue several Church members who had been captured and held by Captain Bogart and his armed militia. Two months later he served on a committee supervising the evacuation of the Mormons from Missouri. He signed a "covenant of removal" pledging his property and worldly goods to help the poor and destitute in that exodus.

Vienna Was Married Late in Life, but Her Marriage Wasn't Peaceful

In spite of the virtues of Daniel and Vienna, their marriage seems not to have been happy. In 1839 Vienna received a blessing from the patriarch, Joseph Smith, Sr., using her married name; she also sent her husband and his son off on a mission. In 1844 at Nauvoo, she received another patriarchal blessing from Hyrum Smith as Vienna Shearer and again in 1845 from William Smith as Vienna Shearer; but on January 22, 1846, as the Saints were being expelled from Nauvoo, she was washed, anointed, and endowed in the Nauvoo temple and then assigned to a traveling company different from that of her husband for the westward exodus. From that date forward she returned to using her maiden name.

At age sixty, Vienna drove her own wagon across the plains. Traveling with Captain Charles C. Rich's guard, she arrived in the Great Salt Lake Valley on October 2, 1847, placing her among the first women to complete the trip. She was given a city lot in the Twelfth Ward and spent the first winter living in her wagon at that location. The next year she erected a house.

Daniel Shearer came west five years later and was assigned a lot in the Thirteenth Ward. He erected a separate residence. Twenty-five years later he named Vienna in his will, using her maiden name, and cut her off with only a dollar and twenty-five cents.

About that same time, in November of 1876, Joseph Smith III, the son of the Prophet, came to Salt Lake City to interview several women who had known his father. He was particularly interested in whether his father had ever preached or practiced polygamy. Joseph III remembered Vienna as having been in Kirtland when he was a child, and he described her as "a frequent visitor in our home" particularly when they were living in Nauvoo.

According to his account of their meeting in Salt Lake City, they reminisced for a time and then Vienna spoke "favorably of the plural wife system of marriage." He asked her, if such was her belief, why she hadn't married long ago and become "the plural wife of some respectable high priest or bishop." He says that she answered, "I have never married either as one wife or as a plural one," and that upon being prodded, she went on to admit that his mother had been opposed to polygamy. He reports that she continued speaking of herself, saying that in answer to prayer she had been told "as if an audible voice spoke" that marriage was not for her and that it was better for her to remain as she was. He then cites her as a proof that his father was never involved in plural marriage.

His account of that meeting seems fully detailed, but he and Vienna must have been speaking at odds, either not really understanding each other or simply hearing what they each wanted to hear. He says of the interview, "I need not attempt to relate all the communication which passed between us," and then gives only what supported his position against plural marriage. Extant records are incomplete, but substantial circumstantial evidence shows that while Vienna lived most of her life alone, she was married to Daniel Shearer for a time and was sealed to the Prophet Joseph Smith while he was still alive, probably in 1843. Rumor had linked her to him as early as the Kirtland period. That sealing ordinance was repeated March 28, 1858, in Salt Lake City.

At Age Ninety, Vienna Jaques Addressed a Meeting of 600 People

One blessing Joseph Smith promised Vienna was that "she would live until her soul was satisfied in beholding the glory of Zion." She lived into her ninety-sixth year. At ninety years of age she traveled with John Taylor, Wilford Woodruff, Orson Pratt, and Edward Hunter from Salt Lake City to Provo, Utah, where she spoke to a gathering of over six hundred "old folk." At age ninety-one she entertained a reporter from the *Women's Exponent*, telling her how she milked her own cow and had made sixty-one pounds of butter that spring.

The reporter went on to describe her, saying: "She lives entirely alone, never having had any family, does all her own housework, including washing, ironing and cooking, writes many letters and does a great deal of reading. Sister Vienna is very familiar with the scriptures."

On her ninety-second birthday Vienna was treated to a surprise party. She entertained her guests by reading them the letter she had received from Joseph Smith many years before. At age ninety-three she was honored in American Fork, Utah, and given an armchair. At ninety-four years of age another reporter from the *Women's Exponent* commented on the "erectness of her carriage" citing Vienna's fine posture as an example young girls might follow. Later that same year on December 23, the anniversary of the Prophet's birth, Vienna was seated at the same table with President John Taylor, President Joseph F. Smith, Elder Wilford Woodruff, and many other prominent men and women at a formal event. As an honored veteran she lived to see the Saints firmly established in the west with every indication that her soul was "satisfied." She died February 7, 1884, in Salt Lake City in the home she built on the lot she was given when she first arrived in the valley.

Her funeral, three days later, drew a large crowd including many notables. Wilford Woodruff, who was then president of the Church, was the principal speaker. He praised her for her integrity. Other speakers included President A. M. Cannon and elders Heber J. Grant, C. W. Penrose, and George Hamlin. She was buried at City Cemetery.

Vienna Jaques was described by her contemporaries as "eccentric," "a Woman's Rights champion," a woman of "life-long integrity and many virtues," a "person of marked individuality of character . . . true to her covenants and esteem[ing] the restoration of the gospel as a priceless treasure." She was a woman who knew her own mind, valued her independence, and took pride in her self-reliance. Yet her pride and self-reliance did not inhibit her. She had tasted the famine in the land—the famine described by the Old

Testament prophet Amos as a hunger for the hearing of the word of God. So when she heard of a new prophet, she investigated. When through her own prayers she became convinced of his divine calling, she sought him out. When he asked her to forsake her worldly goods and follow him, she did. Even when events did not transpire exactly as she had been led to believe, she remained steadfast. Vienna Jaques knew how to separate her day-to-day difficulties from the larger currents in her life, and she launched her boat on the mainstream.

The history of Vienna Jaques provides the background of how and why she came to be named in the Doctrine and Covenants. But more than that, it offers an example of how a woman can use scripture to guide her life. From the scriptures, Vienna knew that the Christian churches of her day were not like the church Christ had established. By prayer and a continued study of the Book of Mormon, she recognized the modern prophet; and when he advised her, she followed that advice. Late in her life she continued to be described as one who was "very familiar with the scriptures."

Vienna Jaques Was Asked to Give Money; Emma Smith Was Asked to Give Time, Talent, and Meekness of Soul

Vienna Jaques willingly gave all that was asked of her. Likewise Emma Smith, Joseph Smith's wife, gave all that was asked of her. But what was asked of her was a great deal more than money.

According to the 25th section of the Doctrine and Covenants, it was not by chance that Emma came to play a prominent role in the early events of the Restoration. She was called to be a comfort to her husband in his afflictions. She was also asked to give her time to writing and "much learning," to serve as her husband's scribe, to expound the scriptures, to exhort the Church, and to make a selection of hymns. She was asked to do those things in meekness that she might win a crown of righteousness. In other words, she was asked for nothing less than her time, talent, and meekness of soul.

If that isn't enough to leave one staggered, the 25th section ends with the words, "And verily, verily, I say unto you, that this is my voice unto all," suggesting that what was asked of Emma is asked of all sisters in the gospel. Thus the 25th section may be the most enlightening of all scriptures for women seeking their divine heritage and current purpose.

But as with many sections of the Doctrine and Covenants, the scriptural directive to Emma is instructions—nothing more—leaving the reader with questions: Did she accept the directive? Did she accomplish all that was set out for her? And perhaps more pertinent to others who may follow: How difficult was the task? How good an example was Emma?

As with Vienna Jaques, the answers to these questions must be sought in historical accounts. But in Emma's case, the answers are less easy to identify. Working under extremely adverse conditions, Emma became by necessity a strong, determined woman. Were it not for her distaste of plural marriage and her break with Brigham Young after her husband's death, unquestionably she would be ranked with the great women of scripture. As it is, she has become a puzzle.

She was born Emma Hale on July 10, 1804, the seventh of nine children born to Isaac and Elizabeth Lewis Hale. The Hale family has been described as "proper, quiet, loving Methodists of old American stock." Emma was herself devout. Her father relates that he was converted from deism (belief in a god who does not intervene in human affairs) to faith in Christ by overhearing one of her prayers. She was seven or eight years old and had gone into the woods to pray for him. He discovered her kneeling there and was deeply affected by the sweetness of her petition. In addition to Christian beliefs, the Hale family valued education. Emma received formal training and was teaching at a school near Harmony, Pennsylvania, living at home, when she met Joseph.

Part of the Hale home was furnished as a boarding house. In the fall of 1825, Joseph Smith, Jr., hired on as a laborer to a neighbor of the Hales, Josiah Stowell (Stoal), and took up lodging with the Hales. He soon fell in love with Emma, whom he described as "very beautiful, with large dignified body and bewitching dark-eyes, and also exceptionally intelligent." She returned his affection.

Joseph approached Isaac Hale twice asking for his daughter's hand; he was refused. Joseph was twenty years old, poor and unschooled—reasons enough for her father to find the match unsatisfactory without the young man's accounts of his religious experiences and his ability to use a "peep stone."

In spite of Isaac Hale's objections, the couple continued to meet at the home of Joseph Knight, a mutual friend, and at the Stowell's without Emma's parents knowing. But the meetings were not frequent. Then on January 18, 1827, eighteen months after their first meeting, Joseph and Emma, both of legal age, eloped and were married by Squire Tarbell, a justice of the peace. Emma recalled the circumstances of her marriage years later in a letter to her eldest living son: "I was visiting at Mr. Stowell's who lived in Bainbridge, and saw your father there. I had no intention of marrying him when I left home; but during my visit to Mr. Stowell's your father visited me there. My folks were bitterly opposed to him; and being importuned by your father, aided by Mr. Stowell, who urged me to marry him, preferring to marry him to any man I knew, I consented."

Emma's marriage estranged her from her family—an estrangement that only grew more distant. The reaction from Joseph's family was the opposite. They liked Emma and embraced the young couple. Emma, who had never met her in-laws before her marriage, moved in with them and immediately returned their warm feeling. Over the years she would continue to get along well with them. She admired Joseph's mother and father, and they respected her. Though trials and turmoil would intervene, her feelings for her husband's family, particularly his mother, Lucy Mack Smith, never changed, nor theirs for her.

Joseph took Emma with him to the Hill Cumorah the night he received the gold plates. She waited in their borrowed buggy while he ascended the hill, returning with a heavy object wrapped in a cloth. On several occasions, she helped hide the plates. Once, though pregnant, she rode horseback for several miles to warn Joseph that the plates were in danger.

Emma was Joseph's first scribe and served intermittently throughout the translation of the Book of Mormon, fulfilling the calling she was given: "Thou shalt . . . be unto him for a scribe, while there is no one to be a scribe for him." (D&C 25:16.) Of Joseph and the translation process, she wrote: "No man could have dictated the writings of the manuscript unless he was inspired. . . . When returning after meals, or after interruptions, he would at once begin where he left off, without either seeing the manuscript or having any portion of it read to him. This was a usual thing for him to do. It would have been improbable that a learned man could do this; and for one so ignorant and unlearned as he was, it was simply impossible."

Emma told how Joseph placed the plates wrapped in the cloth on a table "without any attempt at concealment" and went on to describe them, saying: "I once felt the plates, as they thus lay on the table, tracing their outline and shape. They seemed to be pliable like thick paper and would rustle with a metallic sound when the edges were moved by the thumb."

Others Saw the Gold Plates; Emma Never Did

To complete the translation, Joseph and Oliver Cowdery temporarily moved to Fayette, New York, to David Whitmer's home. Emma soon followed. One day as David Whitmer's mother was going out to milk the cow, she was met by Moroni, who, referring to her houseguests, said: "You have been very faithful and diligent in your labors, but you are tired because of the increase of your toil; it is proper, therefore that you should receive a witness that your faith may be strengthened." The angel then showed her the plates. (B. H. Roberts, *A Comprehensive History of The Church of Jesus Christ of Latter-day Saints, Century One,* 6 vols. [Salt Lake City: The Church of Jesus Christ of Latter-day Saints, 1930], 1:127.) Emma was never accorded the same privilege.

The 25th section of the Doctrine and Covenants may allude to her disappointment: "Murmur not because of the things thou hast not seen, for they are withheld from thee and from the world, which is wisdom in me." Still her testimony stands as one of the most complete. She wrote without equivocation: "My belief is that the Book of Mormon is of divine authenticity—I have not the slightest doubt of it."

The Church of Jesus Christ of Latter-day Saints was officially organized April 6, 1830. Emma had not been able to go to Fayette, New York, on that occasion, so the following June she and Joseph visited Colesville, New York, as guests of the Joseph Knight family. One Saturday the men built a dam in a nearby stream to provide water for baptisms. During the night, enemies of the Church tore it down. That Monday, after mending the dam and waiting for the makeshift reservoir to fill, Emma and twelve others were baptized by Oliver Cowdery. Before the services could be completed, Joseph was arrested for disorderliness because he had "set the country in an uproar by preaching the Book of Mormon." Emma had to wait to be confirmed and given the gift of the Holy Ghost. That constant harassment became typical of her life as the wife of Joseph Smith. She moved often, reared a family, supported her husband, and achieved many personal accomplishments—but always under persecutive pressure.

It was shortly after her baptism, near her twenty-sixth birthday, that Joseph received the revelation directed to her (section 25). In that revelation, she was promised that all would go well for her, that she would be blessed, and that her sins were forgiven. She was called an "elect lady" and admonished not to murmur, but to trust in the Lord. No journal entry or letter exists to show how Emma received that revelation — with joy or reverent apprehension — but her actions testify that she gave it great credence. She had already served in many capacities, and she would continue to serve her husband and his cause despite mounting difficulties.

Through the turmoil of those early years during the persecutions and the separations when she often had no home to call her own, Emma was pregnant and responsible for infant children. Her pregnancies were not easy, her deliveries often complicated. She gave birth to nine children and adopted two more. During her lifetime she buried seven of those children, and another became mentally incapacitated.

Emma's first child, a son, Alvin, was born in Harmony, Pennsylvania, just after Martin Harris left with the first 116 pages of the translation from the gold plates. The child lived only a few hours. Joseph had to leave shortly after the child's death and journey to Manchester seeking Harris. He returned with the news that the manuscript had been lost as well.

In Kirtland, on April 30, 1831, Emma gave birth to twins, calling them Thadeus and Louisa. Like her first child, these died within a few hours. Her father-in-law, Joseph Smith, Sr., later noted her heartache in a father's blessing, saying: "Thou has seen much sorrow because the Lord has taken from thee three of thy children: in this thou art not to be blamed for He knows thy pure desires to raise up a family."

The day after Emma's twins were born and died, a new convert, Julia Clapp Murdock, gave birth to twins and then she died within a few hours. Her husband, John Murdock, gave the two infants, Joseph and Julia, to Emma, as they desperately needed someone to nurse them if they were to survive. She adopted them as her own.

Eleven months later, the twins contracted measles. Emma and Joseph were caring for the sick babies when about midnight a mob broke into the Johnson home, where they were staying, and dragged Joseph out and tarred and feathered him. The rest of the night Emma warmed the sick babies and, with the help of others, scraped crusted tar from Joseph's bleeding body. He recovered, but little Joseph Murdock didn't. Dying from the ravages of measles, he became the fourth child Emma buried.

Through all the persecutions and long absences that separated them, whenever Joseph wrote, his letters were touching, warm, and loving. On one occasion he expressed his concern for her health during her pregnancy: "I feel as if I wanted to say something to you to comfort you in your peculiar trial and present affliction. I hope God will give you strength that you may not faint. I pray God to soften the hearts of those around you to be kind to you and take the burden off your shoulders as much as possible and not afflict you. I feel for you for I know your state and that others do not but you must comfort yourself knowing that God is your friend in heaven and that you have one true and living friend on Earth your Husband."

After one such absence, Joseph came home to find that a new baby had been born just before his return. Emma named the child Joseph III after his father and grandfather. At his birth, Emma was pleased not only that she had a healthy child, but that she and her family were able to live in an apartment over the Whitney store, thus having a home of her own for the first time since she had arrived in Kirtland.

Emma Prompted the "Word of Wisdom"

It was while living in these new quarters that Emma prompted the revelation known as the Word of Wisdom. A "School of the Elders" began meeting in a room over her kitchen. One day, after such a meeting, Emma asked Joseph if he and his companions would quit smoking and chewing tobacco. Probably influenced by the Kirtland Temperance Society, which opposed the use of alcohol and tobacco and eating too much meat, she did not feel such habits were becoming men of God. It was typical of their relationship that when Emma spoke, Joseph listened. She modestly explained her influence, saying, "Joseph knew that I wished for nothing but what was right and usually gave some heed to what I had to say." Joseph inquired of the Lord and on February 27, 1833, received the revelation now contained in the 89th section of the Doctrine and Covenants, a far-reaching code of health.

By 1835 Emma was deeply engaged in selecting hymns in obedience to the command given her: "It shall be given thee . . . to make a selection of sacred hymns . . . which is pleasing to me, to be had in my church." (D&C 25:11.) She was helped by William W. Phelps, the Church printer, who contributed several hymns to the collection. Emma had a fine soprano singing voice, but no formal musical training. It is not known whether she wrote any of the hymns herself. Of the ninety hymns she collected, half were borrowed from Protestant hymnals, including many songs still sung today: "I Know That My Redeemer Lives," "How Firm A Foundation," "Redeemer of Israel," "The Spirit of God Like a Fire is Burning," and others. The book was printed and distributed by February 1836, containing lyrics without music, and may have been used at the dedication of the Kirtland Temple.

By June of the same year, Emma had given birth to another son, named Frederick Granger Williams Smith after Joseph's close friend and counselor. Her son, Frederick, would die within Emma's lifetime, but not until after he had reached maturity, married, and fathered a daughter.

Meanwhile, Joseph was so hospitable that the Smith home was frequently inhabited by overnight guests, the needy, and the curious. Emma had little privacy and often found her budget and her energy dissipated by thoughtless guests. But she managed. Perhaps she managed because she understood the need to share her husband. The Lord had explained: "Thou needst not fear, for thy husband shall support thee in the church, for unto them [the Church] is his calling." (D&C 25:9.) Much later in Nauvoo, seeing her still plagued by similar circumstances, William W. Phelps suggested that the problem of so many uninvited guests might be solved by having a smaller table. Emma quickly replied: "Mr. Smith is a bigger man than [that;] he can never eat without his friends."

More serious was the fact that Joseph made himself personally responsible for some of the remaining costs of the Kirtland Temple, and Emma was left to deal with the creditors. In one letter she explained to her husband how hard it was for her to get money to feed the family: "There is no prospect of my getting one dollar of current money or even get the grain you left for our bread, as I sent to the French place for that wheat and brother Strong says that he shall let us only have ten bushel, he has sold the hay and keeps the money. . . . It is impossible for me to do anything as long as every body has so much better right to all that is called yours than I have."

As their life together progressed, Emma often found herself helping to manage her husband's increasingly complicated financial affairs. That he completely trusted her in these matters is revealed in his letters. On one occasion he wrote: "I can think of many things concerning our business, but can only pray that you may have wisdom to manage the concerns that devolve on you." She did manage, but often it was by doing without. But the Lord had asked this of her: "Verily I say unto thee that thou shalt lay aside the things of this world." (D&C 25:10.)

Emma left Kirtland for Missouri with three small children, expecting a fourth. After she met Joseph a safe distance out of the city, they traveled overland in midwinter, dependent on friends, to a new place already in turmoil even before they arrived. In June she gave birth to a son and named him Alexander Hale Smith. By August Governor Lilburn Boggs had issued his extermination order, stating that if the Mormons did not leave the state, the citizens of Missouri would be justified in taking their lives and property.

In November Joseph was taken from his home in Far West and sentenced to be shot in the town square, within sight and hearing of his wife and children. Joseph begged permission to say good-bye to Emma, which was granted. Little Joseph III, Julia, and Frederick clung to his legs. Emma believed she would never see him again. Her composure broke. Then, at the last moment, he was carted off to prison in a wagon, his life spared.

Joseph was imprisoned for five and a half months in a series of Missouri jails, eventually ending up in Liberty Jail, where Emma and her sister-in-law Mary Fielding Smith visited him. Joseph later wrote in a letter to Emma, "Do you think that my being cast into prison by the mob renders me less worthy of your friendship?" Emma answered, "I still live and am yet willing to suffer if it is the will of kind Heaven, that I should for your sake." This, too, seemed to echo, like a refrain, the personal commandments she had received by revelation: "Let thy soul delight in thy husband, and the glory which shall come upon him." (D&C 25:14.)

On February 15, 1839, again in midwinter, with her husband still in prison, Emma was forced to leave Missouri with the rest of the Saints. The trek was organized by Brigham Young, who assigned Stephen Markham to help Emma and her children make the 150-mile trip to the banks of the Mississippi River. She crossed the frozen river carrying her two smallest children, Alex and Frederick; Julia and Joseph clung to her skirts. Inside her clothing, sewn tightly in cotton bags, she carried Joseph's private papers, including the Bible containing his inspired "translation." Joseph had been promised by the Lord that his translation of the Bible would be preserved and protected. (D&C 42:15.) That promise was fulfilled largely through Emma's repeated care.

She and her children were taken in by Judge John Cleveland and his wife, Sarah, at their farm just outside Quincy, Illinois. She was again dependent on friends for food and shelter. Little Frederick was ill, but he recovered. In April 1839 Joseph escaped his guards, made his way to Illinois, and was reunited with his family.

Immediately pressed with the concerns of the Church and the need to rebuild, Joseph designated Commerce, Illinois—"Nauvoo"—as the gathering place for the Saints. Church leaders obtained land, and Emma moved into an existing cabin on a lot near the river. Malaria plagued the Saints that summer, and Joseph became seriously ill. Emma nursed him and many others back to health, turning her home and yard into a field hospital. Among others, she took in the Walker children, brothers and sisters who had lost their mother. In the years that followed, she and Joseph would come to regard the Walker children as their own and often introduce them as their sons and daughters.

When Joseph left for Washington, D.C., hoping to obtain some redress for the losses the Saints had suffered in Missouri, he was concerned that Emma was overextended and negligent of her own health. On November 9, 1839, he wrote: "Get all the rest you can. I shall be filled with constant anxiety about you and the children. . . . I hope you will watch over those tender offspring in a manner that is becoming a mother and a saint. . . . It will be a long and lonesome time during my absence from you."

On June 13, 1840, Emma gave birth to her sixth son. She named him Don Carlos after Joseph's youngest brother. Fourteen months later Don Carlos, the brother, died. A week after that, Don Carlos, the baby, died too. Death was Emma's constant companion in the early days in Nauvoo. Her parents in Pennsylvania died. Joseph's father, Joseph Smith, Sr., died. Samuel Smith's wife died, leaving several motherless children. And death took members of each of Joseph's brother's families. Even as Emma laid her baby to rest in the family cemetery near the Old Homestead House, she was expecting again. This child, a boy, was stillborn.

Emma's Calling As an "Elect Lady"

On March 17, 1842, Joseph organized the Relief Society, and Emma was elected by the women to be the first president of that society. Joseph cited her election as fulfillment of her calling as an "elect lady." He explained that an elect lady was one who was appointed to do a certain work. To Emma's previous calling to expound the scriptures (D&C 25:7) was added the authority to administer to the poor and improve the morals of the community.

Emma applied herself to her new calling with considerable vigor. She gathered food, clothing, and furniture for the poor of Nauvoo. She regularly addressed the new organization, exhorting her sisters to be united in spirit and purpose and to banish iniquity.

In 1842, under Emma's direction, one thousand Relief Society sisters signed a petition addressed to Illinois Governor Thomas Carlin praising Joseph Smith for his virtue. Emma delivered that petition, traveling to Quincy, Illinois, to speak personally to the governor. At the same time, Joseph was in hiding, avoiding old Missouri warrants and those who would force him back to that state to stand trial on those charges. The governor was impressed with Emma. He pledged to use all legal means to protect the Mormons, but that was a shallow promise. Later, as they continued to correspond, he continued to regard her with respect, but he also expressed his dilemma. He could not recommend that her husband go to Missouri, but duty demanded that he honor requests from other states for the return of fugitives.

While Joseph was in hiding, Emma maintained contact with him through letters and couriers. Sometimes he would slip home. Other times she met him in secret hideouts. He went to Wisconsin for six months and wrote her to be ready to join him. Perhaps remembering the Lord's admonition that she should "go with him at his time of going," (D&C 25:6) she replied,"I am ready to go with you if you are obliged to leave."

In September 1842 Emma nearly died. Her health had not been good since the delivery of her stillborn child, but the Lord had also promised her that her life would be preserved. (D&C 25:2.) She recovered, and the Missouri extraditions proceedings that had kept Joseph in hiding were resolved for a time. Joseph came home. On their sixteenth wedding anniversary, they hosted a party, serving dinner to seventy-four guests.

When the Lord Spoke a Second Time, He Asked That Emma Prove Herself As Abraham (and Sarah) of Old

› By the spring of 1843, the practice of plural marriage had become an issue in Emma's life. It would lead to her being included a second time in the Doctrine and Covenants as part of section 132. Again, the instructions were explicit and demanding. In the 132nd section she was asked to prove herself as Abraham (and Sarah) of old (D&C 132:51), to receive all things, to cleave to her husband and to forgive him. Documents and letters suggest that Joseph had received a revelation on plural marriage as early as 1831 but that his understanding of the principle evolved over several years. Until 1842 he was signing his letters to Emma, "Your Husband until death," or with similar phrases. After that, his letters begin to hint at an eternal relationship. From the first, he privately taught his "new order of marriage" to selected individuals, which probably included Emma; but from the first, she was uncomfortable with the doctrine.

According to the 132nd section, Joseph had been concerned about the proper form of marriage. In the Book of Mormon, Nephi's brother Jacob prohibited his people from having many wives and concubines, calling such practices an abomination because of the sorrows they caused God's daughters. (Jacob 1:15-16; 2:24-35.) Yet many of the prophets of the Old Testament had had more than one wife. In an attempt to understand these conflicting practices, Joseph sought the Lord and was told to prepare to receive the "new and everlasting covenant of marriage." He was also warned that those who received this law were expected to obey it.

Briefly stated, Joseph was told that all vows were of no effect beyond the grave unless sealed by the Holy Spirit of Promise. Those who married without being sealed were not married after death, but were appointed angels, ministering servants, to those more worthy of exaltation. Those who abided the law were promised thrones, kingdoms, principalities, powers, and dominions, and that they would be as gods.

The revelation explained that Abraham had received this law and was already seated on a throne. Joseph was told that the prophets of old had done only as they were commanded and that many had already entered into their exaltation, David being an exception because he had sinned in taking Bathsheba, Uriah's wife. (D&C 132:39.) The revelation then addressed Emma, explaining that she and her husband were being tested as Abraham had been tested. (D&C 132:51.) Then in strong language, she was commanded as "mine handmaid" to cleave to her husband or be destroyed. She was asked to forgive Joseph his trespasses that she might be forgiven her own. In the end she was offered a promise: "I, the Lord thy God, will bless her, and multiply her, and make her heart to rejoice."

Emma's willing participation was fundamental and therefore of concern to Joseph. Ideally the law could not be fulfilled without the first wife's consent: "God commanded Abraham, and Sarah gave Hagar to Abraham to wife. And why did she do it? Because this was the law." (D&C 132:34.) "And again as pertaining to the law of the priesthood . . . [if] the first give her consent . . . then is he justified." (D&C 132:61.) But if a husband taught the principle to his first wife and she refused consent, then he was justified, having met his obligation by his teaching her. He was therefore exempt from the "law of Sarah." (D&C 132:64.) Emma had no choice — either way plural marriage would be a reality in her life. But Joseph's choices were not easy either. He loved Emma, and he was a prophet commanded to obey or be "destroyed." He had taught his wife, and she had refused to accept. Having fulfilled his obligation by teaching her, he may have felt he had no other choice but to go forward with the practice.

By this time Emma had completed most of what had been asked of her in the revelation contained in section 25. Now more was being asked, and she struggled. Her soul was tried, but she surmounted the obstacle, at least briefly. By that fall she had become reconciled to the new instructions, and Joseph initiated her into the endowment, making her the first woman to receive that sacred ordinance. Then she vacillated. Before Joseph's death, she again opposed the practice of plural marriage. Yet, significantly, this was the only doctrine Joseph taught that she could not accept, and she never cast aspersions on her husband's divine calling, never denied her testimony of the restoration of the gospel or the origin of the Book of Mormon. Even years later, still uncomfortable with polygamy, she would attest to Joseph as a prophet and to the Book of Mormon as divine in origin.

In early June 1844, Emma was three months pregnant, and Joseph had been charged with riot in the destruction of the anti-Mormon newspaper *The Nauvoo Expositor*. He talked of going west but returned to Nauvoo from "safety" across the river in Iowa, and Emma remembered, "I felt the worst I ever felt in my life." By June 27, Joseph was dead—murdered in Carthage.

Immediate concern centered on the bodies of Joseph and his brother Hyrum. Afraid that the mobs might desecrate them, Emma arranged to have them buried secretly in the unfinished basement of the Nauvoo House. The demands placed on Emma in the year after Joseph's death were enormous. She was responsible for her own five children and, at various times, a household of other people. These included Joseph's aging mother; Lorin Walker and his new wife Lovina (Hyrum's daughter); William Smith, Joseph's only surviving brother, and his deathly ill wife; other members of the Smith family, including the surviving family of another brother, Samuel, who died a few weeks after Joseph and Hyrum; Wesley Knight and Nancy Carter, two hotel staff members

who had become like family members; and several other
needy individuals for whom Joseph and Emma had assumed
responsibility.

In November 1844, five months after Joseph's death,
Emma gave birth to her last child, a son named David Hyrum
Smith. All Nauvoo celebrated his safe birth. David would
grow to maturity and become a poet, painter, and expressive
musician. His brother Joseph III would describe him as "Israel's sweet singer." But later in his life he slipped into in-
sanity, and Joseph III found it necessary to commit him to
an asylum.

Just Before Joseph's Death
Emma Expressed Her Desire
to Act in Unison with Her Husband

Perhaps anticipating the impending crisis of her husband's
death, Emma had asked Joseph for a special blessing. Tradition places this event just before he went to Carthage.
Evidencing the complete confidence and respect he maintained for her to the end, he told her to compose the finest
blessing she could, and he would sign it when he returned.
He never returned, but she wrote the blessing: "I desire with
all my heart to honor and respect my husband as my head,
ever to live in his confidence and by acting in unison with
him retain the place which God has given me by his side."

For seventeen and a half years Emma stood by Joseph as
his partner in the restoration of the gospel. Yet because of
the difficulty of settling Joseph's estate and what came to be
perceived as her refusal to support the Twelve, especially
Brigham Young, Emma's faith and honor came to be questioned. In fact, for many years it was popularly assumed that
she had failed to live up to her righteous obligations, making
effective the worst of God's warnings to her. (See D&C
132:54.) But as she was warned "to forgive" to "be forgiven,"
so modern historical research has suggested a less judgmental
view. Much of the criticism of Emma may be the result of
misunderstanding.

Emma and Joseph had struggled with financial difficulties throughout their marriage. As early as their Kirtland days, Emma had taken in boarders whenever the family finances were low. At other times, Joseph had casually assumed the debts of the Church as his personal obligations and used Church funds to build the house where he and Emma lived at the time of his death.

Settling his estate under those circumstances made conflict almost inevitable. Emma, as the widow, facing the responsibility of five children and a household of other dependents, needed what she must have felt were rightfully hers—the fruits of her husband's work and her own labors. Brigham, the successor, had to account to thousands of Church members whose tithing and labor had helped build Nauvoo. He must have felt obliged to preserve what he thought belonged to the Church. Before the estate was settled, both Emma and Brigham felt that they had been wronged by the other. Yet seemingly neither intended malice. Both were caught by circumstances and pressured by the events that followed Joseph's death, not the least of which was the forced exodus of the Saints from Nauvoo.

Before leaving for the West, Brigham and the Twelve did what they considered "the decent thing." They deeded some property to Emma for her support. That action led them to believe that she had sufficient for her needs. In actuality, Emma was forced to sell that property at far less than its value to pay creditors who had filed court claims against her. Brigham probably never realized that aspect of her financial plight. After the Mormon exodus, no Church trustee remained in Nauvoo to witness the frustration of the people who stayed behind.

But Brigham was also frustrated. He needed the support of the Prophet's wife, and he never got it. In fairness, it must be noted that although Emma did not support Brigham Young as the successor to Joseph, she did not actively support any other contender. She realized that her son was too young to assume leadership of the Church. Although she took William, Joseph's only surviving brother, into her home after he was excommunicated, she never supported his position either. Yet because of her close connection with Joseph and Joseph's family and the restoration of the Church, a perceived authority rested with her. By staying behind in Nauvoo, she helped create another camp, whether she intended that or not.

On December 23, 1847, Emma married again. Her second husband, Lewis C. Bidamon, known as the Major, was forty-three years old, "handsome, well-dressed, with an easy sense of humor." He was not a member of the church Joseph founded, but he had sided with the Mormons during the difficulties in Nauvoo. Once, acting in the governor's name, he had delivered orders to the commander of the state militia to control the mobs, and on another occasion he was jailed with other supporters of the Mormon position.

Even at the time, some suggested this was a marriage of convenience, Emma being lonely and having considerable property to manage, and the Major being interested only in her wealth. But the letters Emma and the Major exchanged while he was in the California gold fields suggest real affection. They both contributed to the support of the family. She ran the Mansion House as a hotel. Among other things, he worked for the railroad, founded a match company, became a wine grower, and farmed. That he was a respected member of the community is shown in the fact that he won election repeatedly to two local offices. Except for short separations while he was in California and while he fought in the Civil War, they remained together thirty-two years until her death.

That is not to say that Emma's life as Mrs. Bidamon was without heartache. In 1864, after having been married to Emma for seventeen years, Lewis Bidamon sired a son with Nancy Abercrombie, a widow who lived nearby. When this son, named Charles, was four years old, Emma took him into her home at his mother's request and reared him as her own. As Joseph's wife, Emma had adopted twins and taken in and reared several other children. Throughout her life, she had cared for a number of elderly persons as well. That she adopted this last child shows that her capacity for generosity had not dimished with age. And Charles grew up to write a moving testimonial of the love Emma had shown him, saying, "I never heard her say an unkind word or raise her voice in anger or contention."

In 1879 when Emma was on her deathbed, Joseph III came to Nauvoo to be with her. He noted in his journal that he found his brother Alex and his sister Julia caring for their mother and "Mrs. Abercrombie doing the work of the house." Evidently Emma's generosity had extended to Charles's mother, too.

While some would have preferred for Emma to have gone West with the main body of the Church and perhaps played some important role in establishing the Saints in the Salt Lake Valley, she chose not to. Instead, she spent the second half of her life as a quiet, private citizen functioning as the proprietor of the principle hotel in Nauvoo. On April 30, 1879, in the new home Lewis Bidamon had built for her, Emma died, calling out Joseph's name. At her bedside were her two eldest sons. She was seventy-five years old.

All Righteous Women
Are "Elect Ladies"

In the 25th section of the Doctrine and Covenants, Emma was called an "elect lady." Only one other "elect lady" is found in scripture, the unknown woman addressed by John in his second epistle. More interesting are the striking parallels found throughout D&C 25 and 2 John. Both scriptures are addressed to a particular woman and give warm, personal advice to that particular woman. Both scriptures also include the suggestion that what is good for these "elect ladies" may be good for all God's daughters. John ends his epistle by sending greetings to his "elect lady" from her "elect sister," suggesting a broad application for the term. Likewise in 2 John and again in D&C 25, the women addressed are warned not to be deceived, "that we lose not those things which we have wrought, but that we receive a full reward." (2 John 8.)

For both Emma Smith and Vienna Jaques, fulfilling the commands given specifically to them and claiming their promises took extended effort, effort that tried the depths of their souls, effort that took years. In that sense, their examples are worthwhile and distinctive among women named in scripture. Because of a lack of other historical sources, women named in the Bible and other books of scripture often seem remote, untouched by the day-to-day disappointments — not so, the women named in the Doctrine and Covenants, where even Eve is described as being engaged in ongoing responsibilities. That attention to day-to-day living punctuates the Doctrine and Covenants, making divine expectations seem, if not easy, at least possible. For that reason, though the references to women are few, today's sisters can approach the most modern scripture — the one most addressed to this dispensation — as a guide that is both inspired and highly practical.

References

Widows in Scripture
Genesis 38:8, 11, 14, 19; Exodus 22:22, 24; Leviticus 21:14; 22:13; Numbers 30:9; Deuteronomy 10:18; 14:29; 16:11, 14; 24:17, 19-21; 25:5; 26:12-13; 27:19; Ruth (entire); 2 Samuel 14:5; 20:3; 1 Kings 7:14; 11:26; 17:9-10, 20; Job 22:9; 24:3, 21; 27:15; 29:13; 31:16; Psalms 68:5; 78:64; 94:6; 109:9; 146:9; Proverbs 15:25; Isaiah 1:17, 23; 9:17; 10:2; 47:8-9; 54:4; Jeremiah 7:6; 15:8; 18:21; 22:3; 49:11; Lamentations 1:1; 5:3; Ezekiel 22:7, 25; 44:22; Zechariah 7:10; Malachi 3:5; Matthew 23:14; Mark 12:40-43; Luke 2:37; 4:25-26; 7:12; 18:3, 5; 20:47; 21:2-3; Acts 6:1; 9:39, 41; 1 Corinthians 7:8; 1 Timothy 5:3-16; James 1:27; Revelation 18:7; 2 Nephi 19:17; 20:2; Mosiah 21:9-10, 17; Alma 28:5; 3 Nephi 24:5; Mormon 8:40; Moroni 9:16; D&C 83 (entire); 123:9; 136:8

Eve
D&C 20:18-20; 138:39; see also Genesis 1, 2, 3, 4; 5:1-2; 2 Corinthians 11:3; 1 Timothy 2:13; 1 Nephi 5:11; 2 Nephi 2:18-25; Mosiah 16:3; Alma 12:21, 26; 42:2, 7; Helaman 6:26; Ether 8:25; Moses 2:27; 3:21-25; 4:6-27; 5:1-27; 6:2, 9; Abraham 4:27-31; 5:14-21

Vienna Jaques
D&C 90:28-31

Emma Hale Smith Bidamon
  D&C 25 (entire section); 109:69; 122:6; 132:51-56, 64-65; Joseph
Smith—History 2:57-58, 61-62, 75

Bibliographical Note
Information on Vienna Jaques was drawn from Church archive
sources and other historical records; also *Women's Exponent* 7 (July
1, 1878): 20; 8 (June 15, 1879): 12; 8 (July 1, 1879): 20-21; 9 (June 15,
1880): 13; 9 (January 1, 1881): 116; 12 (March 1, 1884): 152; "Extracts
from H. C. Kimball's Journal," *Times and Seasons* 6 (March 15, 1845):
838-40; Joseph Smith, *History of the Church* 1:342, 368, 407-8; and
Saints Herald, October 15, 1935, p. 1329. See also Elder's Licenses
1836-46, p. 14; PB 41:251; 5:113; Nauvoo Temple Endowment Reg-
ister 179, 285; Journal History, June 21, 1847, p. 50; Salt Lake City
Cemetery Book A, 1848-90. Copy of Daniel Shearer will dated July
20, 1843, Salt Lake City, provided by Sherwin Chase of Santa Bar-
bara, California.
  Information on Emma Hale Smith Bidamon was drawn from
Linda King Newell and Valeen Tippetts Avery, *Mormon Enigma:
Emma Hale Smith* (New York: Doubleday, 1984) and the following
articles by them: "The Lion and the Lady: Brigham Young and
Emma Smith," *Utah Historical Quarterly,* vol. 48 no. 1 (Winter 1980);
"Lewis C. Bidamon, Stepchild of Mormondom" *BYU Studies,* vol.
19 no. 3 (Spring 1979); "Sweet Counsel and Seas of Tribulation:
The Religious Life of the Women of Kirtland," *BYU Studies,* vol.
20 no. 2 (Winter 1980); and Linda King Newell,"The Emma Smith
Lore Reconsidered," *Dialogue,* vol. 17 no. 3 (Fall 1984); also Buddy
Youngreen, *Reflections of Emma* (Orem, Utah: Grandin Book Co.,
1982) and Donna Hill, *Joseph Smith, The First Mormon* (Garden City,
N.Y.: Doubleday, 1977). The author also acknowledges the comments and suggestions of Linda King Newell, Valeen Tippetts Avery, and Richard Lloyd Anderson.

3

Joseph Smith's Three Sisters and His Mother

The loyalty of Joseph Smith's brothers, who, like his sisters, are briefly named in scripture, is widely known. The devotion of Hyrum, who died with the prophet at Carthage, and Samuel, who was the restored gospel's first missionary, have become almost legendary. Alvin died young, before the Church was organized, but figured in several of Joseph's visions. William and Don Carlos served their brother in a variety of ways. For example, Don Carlos was associate editor of the Nauvoo *Times and Seasons* when he died, three years before the Prophet's martyrdom; and William, the only brother to long survive the Prophet, was in the East serving a mission when Joseph was killed.

The contributions of Joseph's sisters are less well known, yet they also devoted their lives to the gospel cause, maintaining from the time Joseph first spoke of having seen a vision to their deaths that their brother was divinely inspired. With their husbands and children, they followed Joseph from frontier outpost to frontier outpost, suffering persecutions and dire physical hardships along the way. They hid the plates, stood up to armed mobs, helped construct the Kirtland temple, comforted the sick, and cared for their aged parents, all while maintaining households and bearing children. Often they were alone, their husbands serving missions or away on other Church business. In ways hard to enumerate, Joseph's sisters created the connecting fabric that shaped and supported the epochal events surrounding the Restoration. Dying a martyr's death is dramatic and not to be underestimated, but, as survivors, Joseph's sisters made the sustained sacrifice required of those bringing forth the gospel in the latter days.

Joseph had three sisters. Sophronia, born in Tunbridge, Vermont, May 16, 1803, was two years older than the Prophet. Katherine, born in Lebanon, Vermont, July 8, 1812, was seven years younger. Lucy was the youngest of the Smith family and was sixteen years younger than Joseph. She was born July 18, 1821, in Palmyra, New York, more than a year after Joseph's first vision.

Like sisters everywhere, they shared diversities and similarities. Sophronia has been described as "tall and delicate . . . with soft brown hair and dark-brown eyes." She was said to have been "modest and shy." Katherine was "sturdy . . . with bright expressive eyes" and was described as "a sorrowful child" by her father; as "defiant" by others. Lucy, while sharing her mother's name, was said to have shared her father's mild disposition, being described as a "most pleasant-mannered woman." All were courageous and aggressive in maintaining their faith and upholding the highest moral standards for themselves and their families.

Their mother, Lucy Mack Smith, taught her daughters to be highly skilled in the domestic arts. At an early age, they learned to spin, weave, sew, knit, and contribute in other substantial ways to the welfare of the family. The elder daughters cared for the younger children. The entire Smith household expressed the work ethic typical of New England families of that day, with each child willingly sharing in the efforts of earning a living. The family also shared daily devotions, including prayer and Bible reading.

Prayer Saved Sophronia

According to Lucy Mack Smith, it was prayer that saved Sophronia in 1811 when she was eight years old. A typhus epidemic swept through Lebanon, Vermont, and Sophronia was the first to take sick. One by one the others in the family fell victim to the same illness, but Sophronia's was the most severe. Nearly despairing for their daughter's life, her parents clasped hands and prayed until they received an assurance that she would be spared. Then Lucy Mack Smith picked up her daughter and paced the floor until little Sophronia sobbed and started breathing more freely. Relying on the Lord in times of trouble and uncertainty was a Smith family trait and would be one of the most valuable lessons their mother would teach both her sons and her daughters.

In the religious fervor that swept through New England in the early 1800s, Sophronia joined the Presbyterian Church along with her mother and her brother Samuel. Later when her brother Joseph explained how in answer to prayer he had come to know for himself that Presbyterianism was not true, she switched her allegiance and looked to him for guidance. At first Joseph shared his enlightenment freely both inside and outside the family, but that brought immediate disapproval from the preachers in the area and led to ostracism and abuse. No doubt Sophronia felt those early persecutions as keenly as anyone. She was seventeen and undoubtedly looked forward to being courted. But her friends turned against her, and she grew thin and pale until the family feared she might be developing "quick consumption," a fatal illness common in that damp climate. Ironically, it was her elder brother Alvin who fell ill and died, leaving the family bereaved.

In 1827 Joseph married Emma Hale and brought his new bride home with him to live in rooms prepared for him by his mother and sisters. That same year, he obtained the gold plates he had been commissioned by the angel Moroni to translate. Once he had the plates, his persecutors formed mobs determined to wrest the gold from him for the value it represented. His enemies began to follow his every move. One night as Joseph was bringing the plates home to work on the translation, two men followed him. Hearing a commotion, Katherine, who was then fifteen, ran to the door just as he arrived out of breath. He pushed a bundle into her arms and said, "Take these quickly and hide them"; then he disappeared outside into the darkness. Katherine closed the door and carried the plates back to the bedroom, which she shared with Sophronia. Her elder sister threw back the bedcovers, and Katherine placed the bundle containing the plates between them. Then they both lay down on the bed and pretended to sleep. The men, failing to find Joseph outside, returned to the house and searched through it, but they did not disturb the girls, thinking they were asleep.

The Smith family hired a young carpenter named Calvin Stoddard to finish the house they were building. When Joseph and his father left to go to Harmony on business, just before the final payment on the farm was due, Stoddard convinced the land agent that the two had run away to avoid paying. Then he offered to pay the full price, and he received the deed. Eventually the farm was sold to a third party who allowed the Smiths to continue working the land as tenants.

Ironically, Calvin Stoddard became romantically interested in Sophronia. On December 2, 1827, he and Sophronia were married and moved into a house not far from the Smith's farm. Sophronia was then twenty-four years old.

Following the land incident and whatever amends were made, Sophronia and her new husband remained close to the Smith family. Joseph stopped on his way to Kirtland and preached at the Stoddard home, baptizing several people into the Church on that occasion. When Father Smith was arrested and imprisoned on a debt charge, Mother Lucy Mack Smith suddenly found herself alone, all her sons being gone for one reason or another. She writes that at midnight Calvin and Sophronia arrived at her house. Calvin explained that he had been troubled all afternoon with concern for her. Finally at evening he told Sophronia that he would make the trip to her father's house if she would go with him. Samuel also arrived late that night after walking twenty-five miles, and together they were able to help the Smith parents in their difficulty.

When the Church was organized in 1830, Sophronia and her husband were among the first to join. Katherine and Lucy were also baptized, along with the other members of the Smith family. Then Joseph took his young wife, Emma, and moved to Kirtland, Ohio, where a large congregation had been converted. Directed by revelation, Joseph advised the believers in New York and other New England areas, including his father's family, to prepare to gather to that same area of Ohio. Father Smith had gone ahead. The rest of the Smith family, including Sophronia and her husband, arrived in Kirtland in the early spring of 1831.

In Kirtland, Katherine met an enthusiastic young convert named Wilkins Jenkins Salisbury. He was a lawyer, but he also worked at the blacksmith trade. They were married June 8, 1831, in Kirtland at Sophronia's home. The marriage was performed by Sidney Rigdon.

Together Joseph's Sisters
Helped Build the Kirtland Temple

While in Kirtland, Joseph's sisters helped other Saints moving into the area. They also helped build the temple and became involved in all aspects of life among the converts of the growing church. Meanwhile, their families were growing as well. Katherine gave birth to two daughters and a son. Sophronia gave birth to two daughters. But shortly after giving birth to her second child, Sophronia became seriously ill. A cold developed into "quick consumption," and her family again despaired for her life. The priesthood had been restored, and so this time, besides having the faith and prayers of her parents, she benefited from the laying on of hands. Before receiving this ordinance, she was so weak she could not speak. After receiving it, she told her mother, "I shall get

well—not suddenly, but the Lord will heal me gradually."
She recovered in exactly that fashion. Lucy, Sophronia's
youngest sister, helped with the babies while she regained
her strength.

In 1833 the building of the Kirtland Temple began. A lack
of building materials caused a delay. The construction work-
ers required warm clothing to continue their work into the
winter months. Sophronia and Katherine organized the
Church women into groups, centrally located several looms,
and oversaw the carding, spinning, and knitting of clothing
for the temple construction crews.

Sophronia and Katherine's husbands were also involved
in Church affairs. Katherine's husband was away on a mission when work on the temple first began. He returned and,
seeing that wagons were needed for the work, began man-
ufacturing and mending them. Sophronia's husband sympathized with Joseph's brother William in a dispute with the
Prophet. Nevertheless, still committed to the belief that the
Restoration was divine, he labored on the temple until he
became ill with tuberculosis. Then both he and Sophronia
found it necessary to let others continue the work as she
cared for him in his illness. The Saints labored three years
to build the temple, dedicating it on March 27, 1836.

Joseph's Grandmother Testified of Him

About the time the temple was completed, during the spring
of 1836, Mary Duty Smith, the widowed mother of Joseph
Smith, Sr., arrived in Kirtland. She had traveled from New
England to see her children, grandchildren, and great-grand-
children before she died. She also told her daughter-in-law
Lucy Mack Smith, "I am going to have your Joseph [meaning
her grandson the Prophet] baptize me and my Joseph [mean-
ing her son the Patriarch] bless me." Mary Duty Smith, a
woman of staunch Puritan background and upbringing, believed that her grandson was a prophet and had restored the
gospel in its original purity. Her grandson reciprocated her

esteem, calling her "the most honored woman on earth." Though family members noted her good health on her arrival, Mary Duty Smith died quietly on May 27, 1836, only weeks later, and was buried in Kirtland just north of the temple.

On November 19 of that same year, Sophronia's husband, Calvin Stoddard, died. It has been reported that "during his closing hours, [he] rejoiced to know that he had lived to see the temple completed." He and Sophronia had been married nearly nine years. They had lost their first child in infancy. Sophronia was left a widow with one small daughter.

Little more than a year after the temple was dedicated, Joseph took his wife and family and a company of Saints and left for Missouri. Land had been bought there for homes, and Joseph saw Missouri as a place of permanency. Some of the Kirtland Saints who had suffered economic reverses and the hatred and abuse of their neighbors in Ohio welcomed the chance to move farther west. A short time later a smaller company headed by Joseph's brother Don Carlos also set out for Missouri. This group included Joseph's brother William, his parents, and Lucy, Katherine, and Sophronia and their families.

The eight-hundred-mile trip was harrowing. They slogged across Illinois on roads mired in mud. Horses went lame and wagons broke. They ran out of money and had to sell some of their goods, including a couple of cows they badly needed for milk. At times, they had to make camp for an extended stay while the men got work and earned enough money for them to continue. Lucy Mack Smith describes pitching tents in the driving rain and having no dry clothing at all. Most of the company walked the entire distance to lighten the loads.

They ferried the Mississippi River, and Katherine, pregnant with her fourth child, became ill on the west side. No shelter could be found except an abandoned hut. There, on June 7, 1838, she gave birth to her second son. Unable to travel, she and her husband, Wilkins Salisbury, stayed behind. He secured a buggy, and, a day or two later when her health improved, they were able to catch up with the main group. When they finally arrived in Far West, they found that Joseph had purchased a tavern house large enough to accommodate his parents and his three sisters and their families until they could find places of their own.

There had been trouble in Missouri before Joseph moved there. The sudden influx of more members into a territory that already mistrusted Mormons soon led to armed conflict. But life went on in other important ways. A young drummer boy shot in both legs in one battle was taken to Emma Smith to be nursed back to health. There he probably met Lucy, Joseph's youngest sister. They would later marry. And Sophronia married a Church member named William McCleary, who, being called on a mission, left his new wife to serve. He would also be the messenger Joseph would send to Captain Babbitt, commander of a company of militia in Ramus, Illinois, asking him to bring his troops to the aid of the Prophet at the height of the difficulties in that state.

Joseph and Hyrum were arrested in Far West and were at first sentenced to be shot. Their sister Lucy and their mother were briefly permitted to speak to them and hold their hands. Just as Lucy was pressing Joseph's hand to her lips, thinking to give him a sister's last kiss, the wagon started up and pulled away. The unauthorized military court had reconsidered and decided to take Joseph and Hyrum to prison rather than shoot them. Eventually the brothers spent six months in Liberty Jail. They were still being held in chains when the other Saints were forced out of the state by Governor Boggs.

Years later Katherine's granddaughter remembered hearing how her grandmother had described the suffering endured in that exodus. She wrote:

> We planned to leave for Quincy as soon as we could make ready, for we were anxious to be free from the land of Missouri where, we felt, we were being so unjustly persecuted. Don Carlos, who was to be our leader again, went in search of

wagons. He succeeded in obtaining one wagon and a buggy into which we crowded all our possessions. Father and Mother Smith, we three sisters and our families, our clothing, bedding, and food crowded into the wagon, leaving the buggy for Don Carlos, his small family and possessions. Thus in the fall of 1838 in the cold and rain, we left Far West for the Mississippi River and Quincy, Illinois.

The first night we spent in an old empty log cabin, eating some cold victuals which we brought with us from Far West. The next day we traveled on, most of us walking. Evening found us at the home of one of our church members, a Mr. Thomas, where we spent a comfortable night. The third day it rained, and when night overtook our little exhausted group we had no alternative but to pay the man from whom we sought accommodations for the night the sum of seventy-five cents for a filthy outbuilding which we cleaned as best we could. After carrying water, searching out wood for a fire, and eating a few mouthfuls of food we lay down on the dirt floor to sleep. Next day it continued to rain and our lodging for the night was about like the last, except that our food was exhausted.

The fifth night we were nearing Palmyra, Missouri, when Don Carlos drove up to father and called out "Father, this is too much! This exposure will kill us all. I shall not stand this any longer. The first place I come to that looks comfortable I shall drive in and ask for a night's lodging." Soon we came to a large farmhouse, and Don drove up to ask for the privilege of staying the night, saying "I have with me my aged parents, who are ill, and a number of women and small children. We have traveled for five days mostly on foot and in rain. If we are to go farther we shall all perish. If you will allow us to stay the night, I will pay you well." The gentleman then said, "Do you think I would turn any human being away from my door in such circumstances as this?"

Here we were offered every comfort: a huge fire was made and water was brought by a black servant. A place was fixed to hang our damp clothing, our sodden cloaks and shawls. In the morning we were fed and given milk for our children. We found our friend to be Esquire Mann, State Representative from a Missouri county, who was not antagonistic to our people, but who was unable to help our cause.

Next morning, although it was still raining, we felt compelled to continue our travels. When we came to within a few miles of the river the rain turned to snow accompanied by a drop in temperature. Shortly the snow changed to blinding sleet. The ground near the river was so swampy that the horses could not pull our loaded wagons. We were all forced to walk except father, who was ill at the time but was able to drive the horses. The move ahead seemed to take interminable hours of sinking in over our ankles at each step.

We reached the river, but to our despair there was no ferry that night. We made our beds on the snow, which was then about six inches deep. There we slept as did many other Saints who were waiting to cross the river. Upon awaking next morning we found our beds covered with a top blanket of snow. Our miseries were heightened by the fact that we could not succeed in our attempts to start a fire. Finally we were forced to give up and resign ourselves to waiting cold and hungry for the next ferry.

Samuel was waiting for his father's family and greeted them on the ferry crossing the river. When they arrived in Quincy, he found them shelter. The Smith families settled into several cabins on a single tract of land. The cabins required repair, but Sophronia, Katherine, William, Samuel, Don Carlos, and their families all moved in, and by February 1839 Joseph and Hyrum had arrived from Missouri, bringing the entire family together again.

The Church purchased a tract of land sixty miles north of Quincy in an area known as Commerce, Illinois, and Joseph immediately began organizing the Saints in that area. He moved his family into a house next to the Mississippi River that came to be known as the "Old Homestead." Father and Mother Smith and sister Lucy moved in with him.

The Smith family and many other Saints experienced repeated bouts of serious illness from the effects of the exposure during the Missouri exodus and from the damp conditions around Commerce. Lucy suffered herself but recovered and is mentioned repeatedly in various historical accounts as one who with her mother, sisters, and sisters-in-law nursed the ill night and day, at one time helping in what became a virtual field hospital in the house and on the premises of the Joseph Smith, Jr., home, where many of the sick were brought.

By 1840 all the Smith families had moved to the Commerce area—then renamed "Nauvoo"—and its surrounding counties. Katherine and her husband located fifty miles south in the town of Plymouth, where her husband found work. Still they remained close. Joseph sent for Katherine and her family whenever there were celebrations. Even in their old age, her children remembered with fondness the holidays they had spent in Nauvoo with their cousins, uncles, and aunts.

The family held a reunion on June 4, 1840, when Lucy married Arthur Millikin. Joseph listed Arthur among his close associates who had aided him in times of trouble, describing him as "a faithful, an honest and an upright man." Others described him as "wonderfully pleasant . . . the soul of honor." Lucy's marriage was considered fortuitous by the whole family and was celebrated joyously.

Joseph Smith Senior Blessed His Daughters

Another more somber family reunion was held in September of that same year when Joseph Smith, Sr., knowing he was dying, asked that his children be gathered. On that occasion Lucy's new husband was sent to get Katherine. She came at once but did not arrive until after her father had died.

From his deathbed, Joseph Smith, Sr., the Patriarch, gave his wife and each of his children a final blessing.

To Sophronia he said: "Sophronia, my oldest daughter, thou hadst sickness when thou wast young, and thy parents did cry over thee, to have the Lord spare thy life. Thou didst see trouble and sorrow, but thy troubles shall be lessened, for thou hast been faithful in helping thy father and thy mother in the work of the Lord. And thou shalt be blessed, and the blessings of heaven shall rest down upon thee. Thy last days shall be thy best. Although thou shalt see trouble, sorrow and mourning, thou shalt be comforted, and the Lord will lift thee up, and bless thee and thy family, and thou shalt live as long as thou desirest life. This dying blessing I pronounce and seal upon thy head, with thine other blessings. Even so. Amen."

Although Katherine was not present, he pronounced a blessing for her that her mother recorded: "Katherine has been a sorrowful child, trouble has she seen, the Lord has looked down upon her and seen her patience, and has heard her cries. She shall be comforted when her days of sorrow are ended, then shall the Lord look down upon her and she shall have the comforts of life, and the good things of the world, then shall she rise up, and defend her cause. She shall live to raise up her family; and in time her sufferings shall be over, for the day is coming when the patient shall receive their reward. Then she shall rise over her enemies, and shall have houses and land, and things around her to make her heart glad. I, in this dying blessing, confirm her patriarchal blessing upon her head, and she shall receive eternal life. Even so. Amen."

To Lucy he said: "Lucy, thou art my youngest child, my darling. And the Lord gave thee unto us to be a comfort and a blessing to us in our old age, therefore, thou must take good care of thy mother. Thou art innocent, and thy heart is right before the Lord. Thou has been with us through all the persecution; thou hast seen nothing but persecution, sickness and trouble, except when the Lord hath cheered our hearts. If thou wilt continue faithful, thou shalt be blest with a house and land; thou shalt have food and raiment, and no more be persecuted and driven as thou hast hitherto been. Now, continue and thou shalt receive a reward in heaven. This dying blessing, and also my patriarchal blessing, I seal upon thy head in the name of Jesus. Even so. Amen."

Those father's blessings of peace, prosperity, and freedom from persecution were fulfilled, but not immediately— not for several years. The three sisters saw their father die in 1840 and their brother Don Carlos die in 1841. Joseph and Hyrum were slain in Carthage in 1844, and their brother Samuel died only a couple of weeks later.

Katherine's Children Abandoned While She Attends Her Brother's Funeral

The outlying areas around Nauvoo felt some of the first effects of the threats of violence and growing resentment against the Saints in Illinois that eventually led to the tragedy in Carthage. Katherine and her husband opened their front door one day and found a notice tacked to it: "Get out or be burned out." Refused work because of his Mormon connections, Wilkins Salisbury was forced to leave his family and go to St. Louis. While he was gone, another family moved in with Katherine to help her with work and expenses. He was gone when Katherine gave birth to a daughter and when she received the news from Carthage on the morning of June 28, 1844, that her brothers had been killed the day before. Not knowing what else to do, she left her children in the care of the family living with them and left immediately for Nauvoo.

The family, afraid of more violence and knowing Katherine's family connections, abandoned her children in the middle of the night. Two days later her children, led by her eight-year-old son carrying his two-year-old brother, crossed the street and asked for food from a neighbor. The neighbor woman fed them, made beds on the floor for them, and let them stay. Her husband, returning late that night, feared that they would be murdered if they kept the children, so the next morning they were sent back to their own home to fend for themselves. Katherine, thinking her children were being cared for, remained in Nauvoo until after the funeral. Fortunately her children managed until her return.

Katherine and her husband moved their family to Beardstown, Illinois, in the summer of 1844, hoping conditions would be safer there, but no one would bring blacksmith work to Wilkins because his wife was the sister of Joseph Smith. So the next summer they moved to Nauvoo, traveling at night on back roads. In Nauvoo they shared a brick house near the river, known as the William Marks House, with Katherine's mother; her brother William; and sister Lucy and her husband. Now that they were together again, Lucy Mack Smith commented that her three daughters were a great comfort to her in this time of trouble. Emma Smith and the other widows of the Smith brothers were also close.

In the turmoil, leadership questions, and exodus that followed the death of their brothers, the sisters expressed strong feelings only about wanting to stay close to their families. Mary Fielding Smith, Hyrum's widow, and Levira Clark Smith, Samuel's widow, took their young families and followed Brigham Young west, but the other members of the Smith family remained near Nauvoo and near one another.

That was not the choice of least resistance. The Mormons who stayed behind were subject to boycott, abuse, and slander. They faced all forms of discrimination both subtle and blatant. Years later Katherine's children would describe the ordeal of going to school and working side by side with the children of the men who had killed their uncles. Her daughter was shot at, and one of her sons narrowly missed being hanged. Forty years after Carthage, in the 1880s, Katherine's son Alvin was killed by a Mormon-hater—stabbed with a bowie knife.

When the main body of Saints left Nauvoo, the economy of the area collapsed, leaving those who remained struggling just to survive. By the fall of 1846, the plight of the members staying in Nauvoo was desperate. Several homes had been burned. Emma Smith rented out the Mansion House and went to Fulton for a short time. Katherine and her husband loaded their possessions on a raft and started down the Mississippi with the intention of going south. Unfortunately, as their raft rounded a curve in the river, it struck a steamboat, and they lost everything they owned. They also buried a young daughter in the river bottom there. Stranded, with no way to go farther, they moved into an abandoned house in Ramus, later called Webster, Illinois, which had formerly been a Mormon community. There Wilkins opened a blacksmith shop. They remained there seven years until October 1853, when Wilkins died.

By that time, Katherine's older children were married and living nearby. Like her mother, she expressed appreciation for the comfort her daughters gave her in her time of trouble, and her sisters were still close. Sophronia helped Katherine's youngest son, who was only three when his father died, get an education. According to an often-told story in Katherine's family, Brigham Young sent her $400, hoping she would use the money to move herself and her family to Utah. She bought forty acres and built a house instead. Whether he actually intended for her to use the money to come to Utah is questionable. On another occasion he sent her $200 and wrote: "I sincerely hope it will prove a blessing to you. . . . The memory of our beloved Prophet is deeply cherished in the hearts of the Saints and for his sake, his relatives and members of his family not withstanding our differences of opinion are kindly regarded."

After the main body of the Saints had left Nauvoo, Sophronia and her husband took her daughter by her first marriage and moved to Colchester, a mining town forty miles east of Nauvoo where jobs were plentiful. Her daughter married a well-to-do farmer in that area; and when her second husband, William McCleary, died, Sophronia spent the last years of her life living with her daughter and her husband. She died August 28, 1876, at the age of seventy-three.

Lucy and her husband also moved to Colchester, where they made their home rearing a family of six children. She and her husband both died in 1882. She was sixty-one years old.

Katherine was the last survivor of the three sisters. She was forty years old when her husband died. On May 3, 1857, she married Joseph Younger of Fountain Green and went to live there. She died February 2, 1900, at the age of eighty-seven, having spent the last years of her life with her son Frederick and his family. She was the mother of four sons and four daughters.

Joseph's Sisters Remained Close to the Smith Family

The lives of Joseph's sisters express more than anything else the remarkable closeness of the Smith family. That family was able to encompass many diverse individuals and remain united, even while sustaining the stress of divine manifestations, persecutions, and economic distress. The fortune or misfortune of one was the fortune or misfortune of all. Occasionally Joseph's leadership was challenged, particularly by his brother William, but never was there any indication that a brother or sister doubted Joseph's divine calling. That bond continued throughout the adult lives of the Smith children when many families would have spun off into diverse paths. Even after Joseph's death, the survivors remained close, drawing together for comfort and support.

When Joseph Smith III accepted leadership of the Reorganized Church of Jesus Christ of Latter-day Saints, following in what he believed to be his father's footsteps, it was only natural that the remaining members of his father's family, who had for the most part remained religiously unaffiliated since Brigham Young led the other Saints westward, rallied to him. That was the Smith family way.

On Monday, January 9, 1843, about eighteen months before he was killed in Carthage, Joseph Smith visited his sister Katherine Salisbury. He was accompanied by Dr. Willard Richards. Joseph described the evening he and Katherine shared. They talked about the days they had spent as children in their father's house and fondly recalled their elder brother Alvin, who had died many years previously. Joseph remarked how handsome he had been and how strong. Of the same evening, Dr. Richards wrote, "While there my heart was pained to see a sister of Joseph's almost barefoot, and four lovely children entirely so, in the middle of a severe winter. What has not Joseph and his father's family suffered to bring forth the work of the Lord in these latter days!"

That incident, perhaps more than any other, expresses the charity of Joseph's sisters. They suffered and they sacrificed, and some days they probably despaired; but no matter the conditions, their support of their brother was unconditional. They were Joseph's sisters in flesh and blood; in purpose and in spirit.

Lucy Mack Smith Wrote More About the Restoration than Anyone Except Her Son

Just as Joseph Smith included additional information about Eve, "the mother of all living," in the Pearl of Great Price and Doctrine and Covenants, he also included information about his own mother in two scriptures, including a vision in which he saw her in the celestial kingdom while she was still alive. (D&C 137:5.) Altogether Lucy Mack Smith is mentioned twice in the Doctrine and Covenants and three times in the Pearl of Great Price—one reference taking careful note of her Mack family descent. (Joseph Smith–History 1:4.) But her importance to the restoration of the gospel and continued significance to members of the Church today goes far beyond those brief passages. Her own writings must also be taken into account.

In 1845, ten years before she died, she dictated her memoirs—including the history of her family—to Martha Jane Knowlton Coray, who acted as her scribe. Lucy Mack Smith's autobiography represents the longest and most detailed written witness to the restoration of the gospel extant, with only the exception of Joseph Smith's own writings. The Smith family were close and supportive. Lucy's account reflects that unwavering devotion. Her book and her letters consistently affirm her son's calling and her sense of the significance of her own role in the work. On several occasions she proudly declared, "I am the mother of the prophet."

Lucy was born July 8, 1775, the youngest child of Solomon and Lydia Gates Mack. Her father was a veteran of the French and Indian wars and participated in the struggle for independence from England. Gunpowder was in critically short supply, seriously hindering General Washington and his troops, so Solomon Mack traveled to Connecticut to learn how to manufacture saltpeter. Then he built up that technology throughout western Massachusetts. Later in his life he worked as a merchant, shipmaster, mill operator, and farmer. He prospered and suffered reverses, including two serious accidents that left him partially crippled. Toward the end of his life, he wrote his autobiography to show how his financial and physical setbacks had led him to higher things. He told how he had searched the Bible, questioned his wife (he called her "his only instructor"), and prayed. He described the joy of his conversion, saying, "Everything appeared new and beautiful. Oh how I loved my neighbors. How I loved my enemies — I could pray for them. Everything appeared delightful. The love of Christ is beautiful."

Lucy's mother is extolled in both Lucy's and her father's accounts. Before her marriage, Lydia Gates was a schoolteacher. When she and her husband moved their family to an isolated wilderness area of New Hampshire, rather than allow her children to be deprived of schooling, she assumed charge of their education. According to her husband, she instructed them in the basics of reading, writing, and mathematics, and she was also in the habit of calling them together both morning and evening for prayer and religious instruction. He adds that "all the flowery eloquence of the pulpit" could not have been as effective as his wife's influence. Lucy's spirituality, fine handwriting, and excellent use of the language attest to the success her mother had in all aspects of the education she gave her children. Joseph Smith, the Prophet, also had the benefit of his grandmother and knew her influence. In describing her married life, Lucy notes, "My aged mother . . . had lived with us some time."

One childhood incident profoundly affected Lucy. Both she and her father include it in their narratives—the miraculous healing of Lovisa Mack Tuttle, Lucy's elder sister. Within two years of her marriage, Lovisa contracted an illness that lasted nearly two years. She grew worse until no one expected her to recover. Then, rousing herself, she whispered to those attending her, "The Lord has healed me, both soul and body—raise me up and give me my clothes, I wish to get up." Though still extremely weak, she was helped to her feet, but her weight dislocated both her ankles. She insisted that her feet be drawn gently in and her joints replaced. Then at her request she was taken across the street to where her father-in-law was sick in bed. She told him to prepare for death. The next day in church she sang a hymn and told how she had seen the Savior through a veil and how he had exhorted her to declare to the people their accountability before God and to urge them to be prayerful. She spoke boldly on the subject for three years until she again became ill and died.

Lucy had another elder sister named Lovina who became ill and died about the same time, facing death with great courage because of the spiritual assurances her sister Lovisa had received. Lucy cared for Lovina during her illness, and when she died, Lucy went to stay with her brother Stephen for a much-needed vacation. It was while she was in Tunbridge, Vermont, at the home of her brother, that she met a young man named Joseph Smith and married him on January 24, 1796. She was then twenty years old.

Lucy and Joseph began married life prosperously. Lucy's brother and his business partner gave her a thousand dollars for a wedding present. She saved the money, having other means to furnish her first household, and Joseph owned a farm near Tunbridge.

Lucy would provide the funds to run her household much of her married life. Early on, she painted decorative oilcloths, and her work was in demand. Later, as a widow, she collected several artifacts, including the mummies the Church had once purchased from Michael H. Chandler but which her son Joseph had given her as a source of income, and set up a museum. She charged a small admission to those who came to see her things.

Not until she had been married nearly ten years and a failed business venture left her and her husband deeply in debt did Lucy use her wedding present to pay what they owed. Then they took their three children, Alvin, Hyrum, and Sophronia (Lucy's first child, an unnamed boy, died at birth), and moved to Sharon, Vermont, where they rented a farm from Lucy's father. Her husband worked the farm in the summer and taught school in the winter. Joseph Smith, Jr., her husband's namesake, was born there, as was Samuel. Then the family moved to Royalton, Vermont, where Ephraim and William were born, Ephraim living only ten days.

According to her own account, both Lucy and her husband had been concerned about religion for several years. Finding the various sects of their day confusing and contradictory, they had turned to the Bible for instruction, believing that the primitive church set up by the Savior was preferable to any then being preached. Lucy recorded several dreams that her husband experienced and considered significant, including one similar to Lehi's vision of the Tree of Life. (See 1 Nephi 8.)

Lucy was also spiritually gifted. During an illness that nearly claimed her life, she prayed all night. She was healed, and she heard a voice speak comforting words: "Seek and ye shall find, knock and it shall be opened unto you. Let your heart be comforted; ye believe in God, believe also in me." She later testified that she had made a solemn vow that night to serve God and comfort her mother, husband, and children, a vow she would keep through poverty, abuse, pain, sickness, and death.

The family moved to Lebanon, New Hampshire, where Lucy's second daughter, Katherine, was born. There, like her mother before her, Lucy became concerned about the education of her children. Hyrum was sent to an academy at Hanover; other of her children were placed in local common schools; and she and her husband, who had taught school in Vermont, seem to have undertaken some of the education of their children themselves. They certainly provided a spiritual example.

When typhus afflicted the family, nearly killing Sophronia, Lucy and her husband clasped hands and knelt together, praying until they had received an assurance that she would recover. When the effects of the same disease left Joseph with an infected leg, they called for surgeons but also relied on prayer in their decision not to allow the doctors to amputate young Joseph's leg.

One reason the family drew close and came to rely on each other and the Lord was their frequent moves. After living at Lebanon, New Hampshire, the family moved to Norwich, Vermont, where Lucy's tenth child, Don Carlos, was born. When the crops failed three years in a row, Lucy's husband decided to move to western New York, where he had heard that wheat was being raised in abundance. He went ahead, sending a man and a team back for Lucy and the rest of the family. When this teamster proved unreliable, Lucy not only took over the team herself for the rest of the journey, but she publicly shamed the man who had intended to rob her and leave her stranded with her children.

The family arrived in Palmyra, New York, and took up farming. It was in Palmyra that Lucy's youngest child, her namesake daughter, Lucy, was born, and it was in Palmyra that her son Joseph began to experience great spiritual manifestations that would change her family forever.

Lucy has been described as "not a large woman," her eyes "keen, clear, and blue, even in old age." Her personality was intense and energetic. She had a keen sense of duty and was known to be impatient with others who were less responsible. Her husband was more mild-mannered and often tempered her, counseling her to patience. But hers was a personality that would give her the strength she would need in the years ahead when she would be forced to rely on her wit, determination, and self-reliance to protect her family.

Protecting her family became a prime concern after Joseph's first vision, and it became even more of a problem as stories of golden plates began to circulate in the neighborhood. At first Joseph told his mother only that he knew for himself that Presbyterianism (the religion she had recently embraced) was not true. (Joseph Smith–History 1:20.) After the visit of the angel Moroni, he told his father everything that had been revealed to him and later that evening told the whole family.

Joseph's father's response was to counsel his son to attend strictly to the instructions he had received. Lucy's response was similar. Indeed, the whole family showed immediate interest and reverence for what Joseph had to tell them.

Joseph's Parents Knew True Spirituality and Recognized Joseph as a Prophet

Joseph's parents were acquainted with genuine spirituality. Lucy had witnessed the healing of her sister Lovisa, had been healed herself, and had had prayers answered directly and miraculously. Her husband had experienced a series of spiritual dreams and also knew the power of prayer. Their religious devotion and sincerity made it unlikely that they could have been deceived about their son's spiritual encounters. The fact that they immediately embraced his visions as truth, respectfully instructing him to carefully fulfill all that was requested of him, shows their solemnity about what was transpiring in their home.

Lucy relates that the family frequently met in the evening to hear Joseph explain the things that had been revealed to him, and he often described the customs and dress of the ancient inhabitants of the American continent. She states that he received additional instruction almost constantly during this time. The family's unqualified acceptance also testifies to the importance they placed on the things being manifest. When the angel would not allow Joseph to obtain the plates on his first try, Joseph was afraid his family would begin to doubt him. Instead, according to Lucy, the family doubled their "diligence in prayer and supplication to God, in order that he might be more fully instructed in his duty and be preserved."

Though the family supported Joseph, there is no indication that their support unbalanced the family's shared affections. Lucy and her husband recognized that their third son had been called to a solemn service, but they did not favor him over their other children. In fact, Lucy wrote candidly that his early childhood was not remarkable and that Joseph was less inclined toward books than any of the rest of her children, but he was given to meditation and deep study.

Lucy Could Tell When
Her Son Had Received a Vision
for He Was Visibly Different

It was Lucy's motherly insights and involvement that make her witness most remarkable. She was able to recognize when Joseph had received a vision. She knew when he had his first vision and "inquired what the matter was." (Joseph Smith–History 1:20.) About one such occasion she wrote, "I was accustomed to see him look as he did . . . and I could not easily mistake the cause thereof." The night that Joseph borrowed a wagon and took Emma to the Hill Cumorah to receive the plates, Lucy spent the entire time in prayer on his behalf, in such anxiety that she couldn't sleep. When Joseph returned, he let her examine the Urim and Thummim. On another occasion, he handed her the ancient breastplate. It was wrapped in thin muslin, and she could easily feel the proportions of it and described it in detail: "It was concave on one side and convex on the other, and extended from the neck downwards, as far as the center of the stomach of a man of extraordinary size. It had four straps of the same material, for the purpose of fastening it to the breast, two of which ran back to go over the shoulders, and the other two were designed to fasten to the hips. They were just the width of two of my fingers (for I measured them), and they had holes in the end of them, to be convenient in fastening."

She experienced both the sorrows and the joys that came as Joseph translated the plates. When Martin Harris lost the first 116 pages of the manuscript, Lucy tried to comfort her son but to little avail. She noted that all the family were in deepest mourning and that Joseph paced back and forth grieving. When he set out the next morning for his home in Pennsylvania, he left with a heavy heart, feeling that all he had prepared for and anticipated was lost forever.

But the whole family experienced extreme joy when Joseph was permitted to begin translating again. Even a lawsuit brought against Joseph failed to dampen the excitement. Concerned because her family had never before been involved in such a court proceeding, Lucy turned to prayer. A voice comforted her, saying, "Not one hair of his head shall be harmed." She was satisfied and says that she never enjoyed a happier time.

When the translation was complete, Joseph sent for his father and mother. They went immediately to Waterloo, New York, to the home of David Whitmer, where Joseph, Emma, and Oliver Cowdery had been staying while they finished the translation. That evening they read the manuscript. The next morning, Joseph took Martin Harris, Oliver Cowdery, and David Whitmer out to a grove, where they were shown the plates by the angel. Lucy says that on coming in, Joseph threw himself beside her and exclaimed: "Father, mother, you do not know how happy I am: the Lord has now caused the plates to be shown to three more besides myself. They have seen an angel, who has testified to them, and they will have to bear witness to the truth of what I have said, for now they know for themselves, that I do not go about to deceive the people, and I feel as if I was relieved of a burden which was almost too heavy for me to bear, and it rejoices my soul, that I am not any longer to be entirely alone in the world."

The following day the eight witnesses were also shown the plates. These included Joseph's father and two of his brothers. Lucy herself immediately accepted the book as scripture. She was baptized the day the Church was organized.

While the Book of Mormon was being translated and printed, the persecutions and legal harassment of Lucy's entire family increased. Usually she was able to endure her hardships with equanimity; but when her husband was arrested and imprisoned, she paused to take stock of her situation. Her sons Joseph and Hyrum were both in hiding because of the recent persecutions. Her son Samuel had taken several copies of the newly printed Book of Mormon and gone east to preach the gospel. Her son William was also gone. She says that, like Naomi of old, she had not even her daughters-in-law to comfort her heart. It was her son-in-law Calvin Stoddard who, feeling uneasy about her welfare, journeyed to her home and helped her in her need.

But usually even under the worst afflictions, Lucy was capable of taking care of herself. She stood off an entire mob one day using bluff alone. Another time, confronted by a group of armed men who had sworn to kill the Prophet and all who believed in him, she faced them squarely and said, "Act the gentleman about it and do the job quick. . . . I should not like to be murdered by inches." They backed down.

Early in 1831, Joseph and his father left for Kirtland, Ohio, to escape further persecution and meet with the growing Church membership there. When spring thawed the Erie Canal enough for travel, Lucy and a company of eighty Saints set out to join them and the rest of the Church. Although at first resisting the responsibility, she soon found herself in charge of the group at the request of the entire company, and just as soon she found herself furnishing food for fifty persons from day to day out of her own funds. She called the company together for morning and evening services and took every opportunity to declare herself a Mormon and preach the doctrine.

"I Am the Mother of the Prophet"

By contrast, many of the brethren in Kirtland traveled incognito because of the persecutions, advising others to do the same. When Lucy decided to travel to Detroit to visit her brother, she did not take well to that suggestion. Hyrum proposed that Mother Smith be allowed to say whatever she pleased and if she got in trouble the elders would help her out. So when a Mr. Ruggles, a pastor of the Presbyterian Church, shook her hand and asked, "Are you the mother of that poor, foolish, silly boy Joe Smith who pretended to translate the Book of Mormon?" she looked him steadily in the eye and replied, "I am." Then she went on to prophesy, knowing that the Spirit of God was on her, that within three years a third of that minister's congregation would be converted to Mormonism, including the deacon; her prophecy was fulfilled to the letter. In January 1833, Samuel Bent, the deacon of Pastor Ruggles' church, was baptized.

Lucy participated in every aspect of life among the Saints in Kirtland. When during the ordinance of the washing of the feet there was a particularly strong outpouring of the Spirit, Joseph sent for his mother. When Reynolds Cahoon proved less than diligent in completing a meetinghouse and school building, Lucy helped raise the money. When the men working on building the temple needed warmer clothes, Lucy and her daughters-in-law and the other women of Kirtland made them. And Lucy often boarded so many houseguests that she was forced to sleep on the floor.

When Hyrum and Joseph returned from Missouri with the survivors of Zion's Camp, they acknowledged that Lucy's prayers had been instrumental in saving their lives. In the midst of that trial, Hyrum exclaimed: "Joseph, we shall return to our families. I have had an open vision, in which I saw mother kneeling under an apple tree; and she is even now asking God, in tears, to spare our lives, that she may again behold us in the flesh. The Spirit testifies, that her prayers, united with ours, will be answered." Joseph added, "Oh, my mother! how often have your prayers been the means of assisting us when the shadows of death encompassed us."

In the summer of 1838, Lucy and her family, including her sons and daughters with their spouses and children, moved to Far West, Missouri. Hyrum and Joseph had already gone to Missouri, Joseph leaving in the middle of the night in the dead of winter to avoid his persecutors. The journey was difficult. The family waded through marshes and were subject to driving rainstorms with no shelter or dry clothes. Lucy's daughter Katherine gave birth, and Lucy came down with a severe cold. On arriving in Missouri, she took the first opportunity to find privacy and pray. She prayed continually for three hours, asking the Lord to restore her health and that of her daughter. At the end of her prayer, she was healed and soon received word that Katherine was much better.

Lucy and her family had known legal machinations and mob violence in New York and Ohio, but nothing like the persecutions they experienced in Missouri. Joseph and Hyrum were arrested in Far West and sentenced to be shot. Lucy and her youngest daughter set out immediately to see them. The brothers were being confined on the back of a wagon, and at first the mob refused to let Lucy approach. She exclaimed, "I am the mother of the Prophet—is there not a gentleman here, who will assist me to that wagon, that I may take a last look at my children." Only then was she allowed to hold Joseph's hand for a few moments. Finally the orders to execute Hyrum and Joseph were remanded. The brothers were taken to prison and eventually to Liberty Jail, where they would remain past the time when the other

Saints were driven from Missouri under Governor Boggs's exterminating order.

Their leader gone, the entire population of the Church in Missouri were plunged into mourning, but Lucy writes that in the midst of that grief she found consolation. Filled with the Spirit of God, she received the following by the gift of prophecy: "Let your heart be comforted concerning your children, they shall not be harmed by their enemies; and, in less than four years, Joseph shall speak before the judges and great men of the land, for his voice shall be heard in their councils. And in five years from this time he will have power over all his enemies." Being relieved in her own mind, Lucy was able to comfort others.

Even after the Haun's Mill massacre, Lucy's husband resisted leaving Missouri, hoping for the release of his sons, but to no avail. Joseph sent a personal message to his father, encouraging him to leave the state as quickly as possible. And so, with only a single wagon for their goods and the household goods of their two married daughters, Lucy and her husband set off for Illinois in February 1839. On arriving in Quincy, Lucy took sick, and her family nearly despaired for her life.

About the time she was recovering, the Church sent a messenger to Missouri. He was unable to see Joseph and Hyrum, and the despair deepened among the leadership in Illinois over this turn of events. Lucy listened to their discussion and then, filled with the Spirit, she declared that she would see her sons before another night passed. Edward Partridge gently disputed her, advising her against disappointment, but saying that if her prophecy was fulfilled, he would never dispute her again.

In a Dream Lucy Saw Joseph and Hyrum Escaping Missouri

That night in a vision while asleep, Lucy saw Joseph and Hyrum traveling over the prairie with a single horse between them. She woke her husband and said, "I can see Joseph and Hyrum, and they are so weak they can hardly stand. Now they are lying on the cold ground! Oh, how I wish that I could give them something to eat!" The next day when Joseph and Hyrum arrived in Quincy, they confirmed that they had traveled in exactly the manner she had seen.

Like Lucy, her husband Joseph took ill during the Missouri persecutions; but unlike her, he never fully recovered. He was able to make the trip to Illinois and help establish his family there, but by late summer 1840 he was dying and asked that his family be gathered. Then, like the patriarchs of old, he gave them all a final blessing.

Lucy records her final moments with her husband: "He spoke to me again, and said: 'Mother, do you not know, that you are one of the most singular women in the world?' 'No,' I replied, 'I do not.' 'Well I do,' he continued, 'you have brought up my children for me by the fireside, and when I was gone from home, you comforted them. You have brought up all my children, and could always comfort them when I could not. We have often wished that we might both die at the same time, but you must not desire to die when I do, for you must stay to comfort the children when I am gone. So do not mourn, but try to be comforted. Your last days shall be your best days, as to being driven, for you shall have more power over your enemies than you have had. Again I say, be comforted.' " Then Joseph Smith, Sr., died September 14, 1840, at Nauvoo, Illinois.

His death was only the first of many that would follow in a short time. By that next January, 1841, Mary Smith, Samuel's wife, died of the exposure she suffered in Missouri. In August 1841 Lucy's son Don Carlos died. A few days later, on September 1, Robert B. Thompson, Hyrum's brother-in-law, died. On September 15, Joseph's youngest child, named Don Carlos after his uncle, died. On September 28, Hyrum's second son, Hyrum, died. And through all this grief, the persecutors and dissemblers and apostates, and all the legal maneuvers by the Missourians to extradite Joseph, never let up.

During those troubled times, Joseph was often in hiding. Still, he worried about his mother. She suffered from arthritis until she was nearly crippled. He suggested that she move in with his wife, Emma. Lucy was with Emma on June 25, 1844, when Joseph and Hyrum were arrested for treason. They were taken to Carthage, Illinois, where they remained in jail for three days until they were rushed by a mob and murdered.

Lucy says that when she heard that her sons had been killed, she immediately thought of the promise she had received in Missouri when another mob had tried to take Joseph's life: "In five years Joseph should have power over all his enemies." She counted the months and realized that the time had elapsed and the promise had been fulfilled.

Lucy Lost Three Sons in Fifteen Days—Martyrs All

Yet Lucy's grief was not complete. Within fifteen days of the martyrdom of Joseph and Hyrum, Lucy's son Samuel also died from an illness brought on by the exhaustion and exposure he had suffered while being chased by the same mob that had killed his brothers. She had reared six sons to manhood and only one remained. Nevertheless, she wrote that she found great comfort in her daughters.

In the leadership controversy that followed her sons' deaths, Lucy seems to have placed her confidence in the Twelve. She observed, "The Twelve, who had also been absent, arrived and assuming their proper places, all was set to rights." She served as peacemaker, often smoothing and bridging the misunderstandings that grew up between the various members of her family and those who assumed charge of the Church.

In 1845, just before the exodus of the Saints westward, Lucy spoke at a general conference presided over by Brigham

Young. She spoke at length, advising the congregation on how to rear righteous children. At one point during her speech, she received a resounding shout from the congregation naming her a "mother in Israel." In her speech she also stated that she felt the Lord would have Brigham Young lead the people away from Nauvoo, and she was willing to go with him under certain conditions.

Lucy, who had followed her son from New York to Ohio to Missouri and back to Illinois, suffering the hardships of frontier life, often living in tents, backrooms, abandoned cabins, or wherever she could find shelter, was willing to follow the Church to the West, but only if her bones would be brought back to Nauvoo and laid to rest next to her husband and her children. Unfortunately, as events progressed, she was never able to go. She stayed in Nauvoo with her daughters and Joseph's widow, Emma.

Four days after Lucy spoke at that general conference, her son William was excommunicated. He was the only son she had left. She did not necessarily think he should be made "guardian" of the Church, which is what he had wanted, but she thought he deserved better treatment than to be cut off, and she sympathized with him.

Independent by nature, she wanted a home of her own and asked Brigham Young for an inheritance. She had lived with or near Emma most of the years she and Joseph were married. Lucy must have felt welcome in Emma's home, but she wanted to be on her own. Taking Samuel's daughter, Mary, as a companion, Lucy moved into the house that had been Joseph B. Noble's residence. Obtaining the house was not easy. Brigham Young had purchased the property and instructed the trustees of the Church to give Lucy the deed and some continued support quarterly each year. But Almon Babbitt and Joseph Heywood, the trustees-in-trust for the Church who were left behind in Nauvoo, didn't want William to inherit property that had been bought by the Church. They told Lucy they would not give her the deed or further support if she continued to shelter her son. She had been receiving food, clothing, and wood from the Church. Deeply hurt, she wrote a long letter to the presiding brethren in Nauvoo, saying that she could not describe her feelings: "You restrict my conscious, put limits to my affections, threaten me with poverty, if I do not drive my children from my doors." They recognized that her motherly instincts were right. She was given the deed without further complications, and together she and her granddaughter managed quite well for several years.

Lucy outlived her sons Joseph and Hyrum by eleven years, alert in mind and body until the end. Toward the end, she lived mainly with her daughter, Lucy Millikin, but spent her last five years in the Mansion House with Emma and her new husband, Charles Bidamon, often receiving visitors there.

In August 1844 Wilford Woodruff stopped to see Lucy on his way to preside over the British Mission. She requested a blessing from him, and he records that she was promised, "When thou shalt be called upon to depart, thou shalt lie down in peace having seen the salvation of thy God who has laid the everlasting foundation for the deliverance of Israel through the instrumentality of thy sons." On May 14, 1856, that promise was fulfilled. Lucy Mack Smith died peacefully in her sleep.

Lucy understood the significance of the restoration of the gospel and her witness to those events. After the deaths of her sons, she began dictating her history, *Biographical Sketches of Joseph Smith the Prophet and his Progenitors for Many Generations.* She may have had some historical memorabilia in her possession, but most such artifacts had been lost in the flight from Missouri, so she drew mainly on her memory. Her memory was good. She is photographic in her recall of scenes and recent studies comparing her account to original documents, which were not then available to her show her to be extraordinarily accurate in her recall of names and episodes back as far as her mid-adolescence.

For a Time Her Book Was Banned in Utah

The manuscript of her memoirs came into the hands of Apostle Orson Pratt in 1852 as he was on his way to serve a mission in England. The book was first published in England without revision under his direction in 1853. There were some historical inaccuracies in what Lucy had written, but more troublesome were the inaccuracies in the Preface written by Elder Pratt. He stated that Lucy's book had been read and approved by the Prophet Joseph Smith during his lifetime when in fact the book had not been started until a year after his martyrdom. For that reason and other financial considerations, the book was disapproved by Brigham Young on August 23, 1865, and the edition was suppressed. According to Joseph F. Smith, Lucy's grandson who was also an apostle and later president of the church, the merits of Lucy's account were "fully recognized by the authorities, many of whom were greatly disappointed at the necessity of issuing the order to temporarily suppress its further circulation." Subsequently the book was revised and reissued in what came to be known as "the Utah edition."

Lucy's account is remarkable not only for its history, the detail and personal insight she offers, but as a testimony that those events were divinely inspired. Mothers usually come to know their children extremely well and are not easily deceived by exaggerated claims. Yet Lucy consistently refers to her son, Joseph, as a prophet of God. Of the Book of Mormon, she writes: "That book was brought forth by the power of God and translated by the gift of the Holy Ghost; and if I could make my voice sound as loud as the trumpet of Michael the Archangel I would declare the truth from land to land, and from sea to sea, and the echo should reach to every isle, until every member of the family of Adam should be left without excuse. For I do testify that God has revealed himself to man again in these last days."

To that she adds testament to her own spirituality. Lucy speaks repeatedly about her prayers and their efficacy. She was healed several times, saw visions and heard heavenly voices. She speaks of such events with reverence and absolute affirmation without any sensationalism and yet with a certain matter-of-factness as though she could hardly conceive of directing one's life by lesser guideposts.

In all, Joseph never had a more staunch supporter than his mother and he reciprocated. On December 18, 1833, he praised his mother saying: "And blessed is my mother, for she is a mother in Israel, and shall be a partaker with my father in all his patriarchal blessings. . . . Blessed is my mother for her soul is ever filled with benevolence and philanthropy, and not withstanding her age, she shall yet receive strength and be comforted in the midst of her house, and thus saith the Lord, she shall have eternal life."

In his vision of January 21, 1836, concerning the temple endowment, now recorded in the Doctrine and Covenants Section 137, Joseph saw his mother in heaven while she was still in her earthly tabernacle. She was in the company of Adam and Abraham, her husband and her son Alvin, who had passed on much earlier. The vision suggests, as Joseph stated in his previous blessing, that she had already earned a place for herself in the Celestial Glory. But one need not be a prophet to recognize that as an accurate estimation of Lucy Mack Smith.

References

Sophronia, Katherine, and Lucy (the Prophet's Sisters)
Doctrine and Covenants 122:6; Joseph Smith–History 2:4, 7

Lucy Mack Smith
Doctrine and Covenants 122:6; 137:5; Joseph Smith–History 1:4, 7, 20

Bibliographical Note
Sources for this chapter include Mary Salisbury Hancock, "The Three Sisters of the Prophet Joseph Smith" *Saints Herald,* January 11, 1954, pp. 34-36; January 18, 1954, pp. 58-59; January 25, 1954; Lynne E. Smith, "The Three Sisters of the Prophet Joseph Smith:

Sophronia, Katherine, and Lucy," Joseph Smith Sr. Family Reunion Booklet, Nauvoo, Ill., 1972; Richard Lloyd Anderson, *Joseph Smith's New England Heritage* (Salt Lake City: Deseret Book Company, 1971); Emma M. Phillips, Dedicated to Serve: Biographies of 31 Women of the Restoration (Independence: Herald House, 1970); Cecil McGavin, *The Family of Joseph Smith* (Salt Lake City: Bookcraft, 1963); Joseph Smith, *History of the Church of Jesus Christ of Latter-day Saints* (Salt Lake City: Deseret Book Company, 1970); Lucy Mack Smith, *History of Joseph Smith by his Mother* (Salt Lake City: Bookcraft, 1979); and Linda King Newell and Valeen Tippetts Avery, *Mormon Enigma: Emma Hale Smith* (New York: Doubleday, 1984).

Information on Lucy Mack Smith was taken from her own writings and other sources, including Lucy Mack Smith, *History of Joseph Smith by his Mother* (Salt Lake City: Bookcraft, 1979); Richard Lloyd Anderson, *Joseph Smith's New England Heritage* (Salt Lake City: Deseret Book Company, 1971); Buddy Youngreen, "The Death Date of Lucy Mack Smith: 8 July 1775 – 14 May 1856," *BYU Studies* 12 (Spring 1972), p. 318; Ivan J. Barrett, "Heroines of the Church," in *Leadership Week Lectures* (Provo, Utah: Brigham Young University, 1956), p. 73.

4

Ancient Women in the
Pearl of Great Price and the
Joseph Smith Translation

Approximately sixty individual heavenly beings appeared to Joseph Smith in the years when he was restoring The Church of Jesus Christ of Latter-day Saints. One was a woman, Eve. In noting her visit, the Prophet said nothing of why she appeared, but in his lifetime, he nearly doubled the scriptural verses referring to "the mother of all living." His additions include the fact that she heard God's voice, taught her children, and expressed her testimony in her own words:

"And Eve . . . was glad, saying: Were it not for our transgression we never should have had seed, and never should have known good and evil, and the joy of our redemption, and the eternal life which God giveth unto all the obedient." (Moses 5:11.)

The addition of information about Eve did not end with Joseph Smith. As revelation in this dispensation continued, Joseph F. Smith expanded on Eve's role. He saw her in a vision engaged in important work at the head of her daughters. (D&C 138:39.)

These references, though brief, give vast depth and dimension to our knowledge of "the mother of all living" and to our understanding of the role of her daughters—a depth suggested only obliquely in the Bible. The restored references to Eve are typical of the changes and additions Joseph Smith made throughout his inspired translation and in other writings, many of which are found in the Pearl of Great Price.

Altogether, a surprising number of ancient women are mentioned in the Pearl of Great Price, given its length. Eve and at least nine generations of her daughters are listed. Sarah, Abraham's wife, is named, as is Milcah, who married Abraham's brother, Nehor. These women are also found in the Old Testament. But the Pearl of Great Price includes five women not mentioned anywhere else and surprising new information on those who are found in other sources.

For example, the book of Genesis mentions Cain's wife as conceiving and giving birth to a son. Nothing else is said of her. But the book of Moses gives the additional information that her choice of evil made her a full accomplice in the events that followed Cain's murdering of his brother. The Pearl of Great Price notes that she was the daughter of one of Cain's brothers and that she "loved Satan more than God."

Cain had made a secret oath with Satan and had come to be called "Master Mahan." When he killed his brother, he was shut out of the presence of God. Fully knowing the consequences, his wife and many of his brothers chose to live with him in the land of Nod, east of Eden. There his wife conceived and gave birth to their son. The Pearl of Great Price also notes that she was the mother of many daughters, and it lists three generations of her granddaughters. (Moses 5:41-43.)

Five generations later, a descendant of Cain named Lamech married two women: Adah and Zillah. Zillah became the mother of a son named Tubal Cain and a daughter named Naamah.

Like his fathers before him, going back to Cain, Lamech entered into an evil covenant and also became known as

"Master Mahan." He killed Irad, his great-grandfather, and then bragged to his wives of his deed, saying that if Satan had rewarded Cain sevenfold, Satan could reward him seventy and sevenfold.

But unlike Cain's wife, Lamech's wives would have no part of their husband's evil. They rebelled against him and told "abroad" what he had said. His secret made known, Lamech found himself cast out and in fear of being killed himself. Then, the scriptures say, "among the daughters of men these things [the secret combinations] were not spoken because that Lamech had spoken the secret unto his wives, and they rebelled against him, and declared these things abroad." (Moses 5:53.)

The Bible ends the story with Lamech bragging to Adah and Zillah. The Pearl of Great Price goes on to describe the choice these women made to expose that evil, and thus offers a far more inspiring story.

Both scriptures list a genealogy of daughters. Adam had many daughters; his son Seth had many daughters; and Seth's son Enos had many daughters. But because of the secret combinations and the wars and bloodshed initiated by Cain and continued by men like Lamech, Enos took the righteous seed of Father Adam and traveled to a land of promise, which he named after his son Cainen (Canaan). Cainen was the father of many daughters; his son Mahalaleel had many daughters; and Mahalaleel's son Jared had many daughters. Jared's son Enoch had daughters mentioned only in the Old Testament. Enoch's son Methuselah had daughters, and Methuselah's son Lamech (not the same as the husband of Adah and Zillah) had daughters who were the sisters of Noah.

Noah's Wicked Granddaughters
Caused the Earth to Be Cleansed

No daughters of Noah are mentioned in the Pearl of Great Price or the Old Testament, but Noah's granddaughters are blamed for much of the wickedness that caused God to cleanse the earth with water. The "sons of men," meaning the descendants of Cain (Moses 5:52; 6:14; 8:14), found Noah's granddaughters pleasing and married them. The Lord told Noah, "The daughters of thy sons have sold themselves" (Moses 8:15), and he threatened to send floods to wash them away.

Noah preached repentance to his granddaughters and their husbands, but they would not listen. The husbands boasted that they were mighty, and their wives (unlike Lamech's wives) loved what they heard and chose to continue in wickedness. They even consented to their husbands' trying to kill Noah. (Moses 8:14-15, 21, 26.) Unable to save his granddaughters from destruction, Noah took only his wife, his three righteous sons, and his sons' wives into the ark.

The women who survived the flood became the mothers of the generations of Noah's family as listed in the tenth chapter of Genesis. No daughters are named in that genealogy. But in the book of Abraham, a granddaughter of Noah is named following the flood, again illustrating beyond what the Bible records the far-reaching influence a woman can have on generations of her descendants.

Egyptus was the daughter of Ham and his wife, who was also named Eyptus. According to the account, she discovered the land of Egypt—a name meaning "forbidden." She settled her sons in that land, and her descendants preserved the "curse" or lineage of Cain with its knowledge of secret combinations and evil oaths. (Abraham 1:23-24.)

The first pharaoh of Egypt was the eldest son of Egyptus. This pharaoh was a righteous man who judged his people wisely. He received many blessings from Noah, but not the conferral of the priesthood. Nevertheless, the pharaohs who followed him claimed that they had the priesthood, and it was the priest of one such pharaoh who killed the three daughters of Onitah.

The Daughters of Onitah Were Sacrificed

The three daughters of Onitah are mentioned only in the Pearl of Great Price, and there only briefly, but their courage is unmistakable. In the time of Abraham, men, women, and children were ritually killed in sacrifice to the Egyptian gods. One day, the priest offered three virgins at once. They were the daughters of Onitah — royal princesses directly descended from Ham and his daughter Eyptus, but young women who knew the truth and would have nothing less. The scriptures say these three young women were killed "because . . . they would not bow down to worship gods of wood or of stone." (Abraham 1:11.)

Immediately after killing the daughters of Onitah, the priest took Abraham, who had been preaching repentance, and placed him on the same altar (a representation of which is given in the facsmile at the beginning of the book of Abraham). The priest would have sacrificed Abraham too, but an angel of God loosened his bands, broke the altar, and killed the priest. Abraham then took his wife Sarah, his nephew Lot, and Lot's family to Canaan, where Sarah miraculously conceived after being past the age of childbearing. Together she and Abraham became the parents of the Israelite nation and the progenitors of the Savior.

Though a great many women are mentioned in the Pearl of Great Price, such as Sarah and the daughters of Onitah, none are discussed in any depth, yet their pervasive influence, for good or for evil, forms the underpinnings of the whole narrative. In brief vignettes, Cain's wife, Lamech's wives, Noah's granddaughters, the generations of Eve's daughters, and the daughters of Onitah all illustrate the lasting effect of the choices these women made. The message is clear. How a woman lives matters not only to herself but to those around her.

With much the same effect, several scriptures about
women are corrected and expanded by Joseph Smith in his
inspired translation of the Bible. For example, in the New
Testament, he notes that *two* angels rolled the stone away
from the Savior's tomb on that morning when Mary Magdalene and the other women came bringing spices.

At first the apostles were reluctant to believe these women
when they told of the empty tomb and the risen Christ. But
God was revealing the greatest of all miracles, and what those
women had seen needed to be believed by all who would
call themselves Christians. So the fact that there were *two*
angels is important because it gives the testimony of Mary
Magdalene and the other women greater validity. Hebrew
law required two witnesses, and both angels testified, "He
is risen; he is not here; behold the place where they laid
him." (JST Mark 16:4.)

Elisabeth Reared John Alone

In other New Testament teachings, Joseph Smith told how
Elisabeth and her husband, Zacharias, saved their child,
John, from the soldiers ordered to kill all male babies in
Bethlehem. Like Jesus, John (who would come to be known
as John the Baptist) lived with his parents near Bethlehem
and was only six months older than his cousin and therefore
in danger. Joseph, being warned, took Mary and Jesus and
fled to Egypt. John's father, Zacharias, being warned, sent
Elisabeth and John into the mountains while he stayed behind
to officiate in the temple. When he refused to reveal the
hiding place of his son, he was killed in front of the altar, a
fact that was mentioned by Jesus (Matthew 23:35; Luke 11:51),
but that is not clearly understandable without Joseph Smith's
additional teachings.

The Prophet's additional teachings also help explain why
John is described as growing up in the wilderness eating
"locusts and honey," the food of the poor. His parents were

prominent in the community and seemingly made an adequate living at the time of his birth. But as Joseph Smith explains it, after her husband's murder, Elisabeth would have been left a widow unable to return to her home. She would have had to rear her son alone in the wilderness, that being the only safe place. That she accomplished such a feat is to her credit.

Likewise in the Old Testament portion of his "translation," Joseph Smith clarifies the role of Moses' wife, stating that *because* Zipporah took a sharp stone and circumcised her child, the Lord spared her husband (JST Exodus 4:25-26), and he mentions Pharaoh's daughter in a lengthy prophecy that foretells her role in saving Moses (JST Genesis 50:29). Joseph Smith revised other passages in significant ways; but more than any other change, the corrections he made to the story of Lot's daughters completely alters our understanding of what happened in Sodom the night before its destruction.

Joseph Smith's Corrections Change the Story of Lot's Daughters

The story begins earlier with Abraham saving his nephew, Lot, with his wife and family several times, including once from an Elamite army that had captured them and all their household. (See Genesis 14:16.) The last time Abraham saved Lot and his family, it was by striking a bargain with the Lord.

Three holy men (actually angels in disguise) stopped at Abraham's tent. Then the Lord appeared and spoke against the great wickedness of Sodom and Gomorrah, revealing his plan to destroy the cities. Abraham, fearing for Lot and his family, who lived there, expressed concern. He asked the Lord if he would destroy the righteous with the wicked. The Lord promised Abraham that the city would be saved if fifty righteous people could be found in it. Abraham continued to talk to the Lord, asking him to spare the city for the sake of forty-five, then forty, then thirty, then twenty, and finally ten righteous people. Each time the Lord agreed.

At this point, the King James translators say that two angels, disguised as men, came to Sodom, where Lot sat at the gate. Joseph Smith says that three angels — presumably the same three who spoke with Abraham — came to Sodom. After being freed from the Elamite army, Lot had evidently returned to live in Sodom and had assumed a position of great stature. "Sitting at the gate" implies an official capacity. The entrance gate of the walled cities of that time was where the market was held and justice was administered. Lot may have been a judge, as he was later taunted with that title. (Genesis 19:9; JST Genesis 19:10.)

Sitting at the gate, Lot met the holy men and invited them to his home, offering to wash their feet and feed them. After some hesitation they agreed, so Lot took them home and prepared a feast. But before they could retire to bed, all the men of Sodom, both young and old, surrounded Lot's house and called out to him, "Where are the men who came to you tonight? Bring them out to us, that we may know them."

Lot went out of his house and shut the door behind him. He confronted the mob, saying, "I beg you, my brothers, do not act so wickedly." Lot was in a difficult situation. He owed his guests protection by any means at his disposal. Because of the difficulty of procuring necessities when traveling, the duty of hospitality was observed with strictness. Lot had taken these men under his roof, meaning that he had extended his hospitality to them with all the obligations that implied. The King James translation suggests that to protect his guests, Lot offered the mob his two virgin daughters. (Genesis 19:8.) Not satisfied to have the women, the mob accused Lot, a foreigner, of trying to be their judge. A scuffle followed, and the mob nearly broke down the door. The disguised angels saved Lot by pulling him back into the house just in time.

Joseph Smith tells the story differently. According to his translation, Lot did *not* offer his young virgin daughters to the mob. No righteous man ever would, and Lot is consistently described as being righteous. According to Joseph

Smith, the mob demanded *both* Lot's guests and his daughters, wanting to sodomize the men and rape the women. Lot protected both his daughters and his guests. He refused both requests. (JST Genesis 19:9-15.)

Sending the angels to Lot's home may have been a final test, for it was only after Lot stood up to the mob that the angels warned him to gather his household, his sons, daughters, sons-in-law, and servants, and flee the city. Lot went out during the night and spoke to his sons-in-law. These may have been future sons-in-law betrothed to his daughters, or Lot may have had other older married daughters as well as the two still living at home. His sons-in-law would not listen. When morning came, the angels urged Lot to forget the others and take his wife and two daughters and flee. Still he hesitated until the men of God led him and his wife and two daughters out of the city.

The angels departed with a warning: "Escape for thy life, look not behind thee, neither stay thou in all the plain; escape to the mountain lest thou be consumed." (Genesis 19:17.) Lot pleaded, as Abraham had pleaded, not to be sent to the mountains but to a nearby village named Zoar. His request was granted.

As Lot and his family entered Zoar, a rain of fire and brimstone descended on Sodom and Gomorrah. But Lot's wife failed to heed the final warning of the angels. She looked back and "became a pillar of salt."

The south end of the Dead Sea contains sulfur and bitumen, which may have exploded through layers of rock salt. An earthquake could have released naphtha and ignited the conflagration. Lingering behind, Lot's wife may have been overcome by sulfurous vapors and literally encrusted with salt. How it happened is not as important as why it happened. Lot's wife as described in that single sentence has come to symbolize all who are so taken up with material things that they cannot avoid destruction. Yet nothing in the account suggests that she was wicked or associated with the wickedness of Sodom. She may have looked back because of the pleasures she had left behind, or because she hoped that her sons-in-law had changed their minds and were following them. Whatever the reason, being warned, she failed to heed the instructions. She was almost saved, but being almost saved was not enough.

With similar words, Jesus warned the followers of his day of the approaching destruction of Jerusalem. He instructed them to flee to the hills when the danger came, telling them not to pause to take anything with them. He added the stern warning, "Remember Lot's wife." (See Luke 17:32.)

Joseph Smith does not add anything to the story of Lot's wife, but he does supply more detail about Lot's daughters. Their mother dead and everything they had known destroyed, they left Zoar with their father and settled in the hill country, making their home in a cave. The elder daughter said to her younger sister, "Our father is old, and there is not a man in the earth to come unto us." (Genesis 19:31.) Then she suggested that they make their father drunk and sleep with him so that they might have children by him. The Bible implies that Lot's daughters thought they were the last humans left alive and that their actions were resourceful— the means of preserving humankind and their father's family under dire circumstances. Joseph Smith, however, adds the words "dealt wickedly" to his description of their actions. (See footnote to Genesis 19:37, LDS edition.)

Taking care not to be perceived, Lot's elder daughter approached her father. The next day she suggested that her younger sister do the same. Both daughters became pregnant. The eldest had a son she named Moab, the ancestor of the Moabites. The younger gave birth to a son she named Ben-ammi, the ancestor of the Ammonites.

Both the Moabites and the Ammonites became enemies of Israel and still God protected them. They were among the first people the Israelites encountered as they neared the end of their forty years of wandering in the desert and started into Canaan. God had commanded the Israelites to "utterly destroy" many of the tribes occupying the land he had prom-

ised to the descendants of Abraham, but he "looked favorably" on the descendants of Lot's daughters. He told Moses
not to displace them or contend with them or even to meddle
with them because he had given the land of Ar to the children
of Lot as a possession. (Deuteronomy 2:9, 19.)

In one of his allegories, Ezekiel describes the other daughters of Sodom, the ones who were destroyed. He names the
sins of the women of Sodom, saying they had too much pride,
too much rich food, and too much ease. They never helped
the poor, and they engaged in filthy sexual practices. He goes
on to accuse the people of his day of having engaged in sins
far worse — sins so bad as to make their sisters of Sodom
appear virtuous. (See Ezekiel 16:48-50.)

Though Lot's daughters grew up in that environment,
they enjoyed many advantages both spiritual and material.
They had a wealthy and righteous father. They had been
saved by Abraham and had heard the warning of angels; but
so had their mother, and she had been lost. They were young,
inexperienced, and faced with what they thought was the
extinction of the human race, so it is easy to make excuses
for them and say that they resorted to actions probably not
unlike what they had seen all around them as they were
growing up. But Joseph Smith, by adding those two words,
"dealt wickedly," makes excuses mute.

Why Lot chose to live and rear his family in Sodom is
never explained in scripture. The apostle Peter described Lot
as a just man "vexed with the filthy conversation of the
wicked." (2 Peter 2:7-9.) Likewise Abraham described his
nephew as a righteous man, and though fewer than ten
righteous people were found in Sodom, the Lord sent his
angels to save Lot and his wife and his two daughters. Joseph
Smith, in clarifying that Lot defended his daughters from the
men of Sodom, corrects that seeming anomaly of a "righteous" father, saved by the Lord, who was willing to sacrifice
his daughters to a lecherous mob. In turn, his daughters
sought to save their father's lineage by taking it upon themselves to give him sons. They were wrong. Still the Lord

seems not to have judged them harshly. He continued to protect the children of Lot's daughters even though they did not prove to be righteous nations.

Joseph Smith grew up in a home where the Bible was read. Undoubtedly he knew the stories of Eve, Elisabeth, and Lot's family from his mother's knee. That he restored lost truths about those ancient women only emphasizes the continued influence their examples exert. His additions and corrections are brief and scattered through the Pearl of Great Price, the inspired translation, and other writings. Yet a theme emerges: How one woman decides to live her life, whether for good or for evil, profoundly affects the generations who follow. And that was a lesson too important to be lost.

References

Eve
Moses 2:27; 3:21-25; 4:6-27; 5:1-27; 6:2, 9; Abraham 4:27-31; 5:14-21; D&C 20:18-20; 138:39; 1 Nephi 5:11; 2 Nephi 2:18-25; Mosiah 16:3; Alma 12:21, 26; 42:2, 7; Helaman 6:26; Ether 8:25; Genesis 1; 2; 3; 4; 5:1-2; 2 Corinthians 11:3; 1 Timothy 2:13
(Reference to Eve appearing to Joseph Smith: see Oliver B. Huntington diary, volume 2, page 244, Brigham Young University Library Special Collections; and list of fifty-nine heavenly beings who appeared to Joseph Smith, compiled by H. Donl Peterson, Religion Department, Brigham Young University; also see his book *Moroni: Ancient Prophet—Modern Messenger* (Bountiful, Utah: Horizon, 1983)

Elisabeth
Luke 1:5-80; Matthew 11:11; John 3:30; D&C 84:27 (see also *Teachings of the Prophet Joseph Smith*, compiled by Joseph Fielding Smith [Salt Lake City: Deseret Book Company, 1938], p. 261)

Zipporah
JST Exodus 4:25-26; Exodus 2:21-22; 4:24-25; 18:1-6

Pharaoh's Daughter
JST Genesis 50:29; Exodus 2:5-10; Acts 7:21; Hebrews 11:24

Milcah
Abraham 2:2; Genesis 11:29; 22:20, 23; 24:15, 24, 47

Cain's wife and the generations of her daughters
Moses 5:28, 41-43; Genesis 4:17

Adah, Zillah, and Naamah (Lamech's wives and daughter)
Moses 5:44-47, 52-53; Genesis 4:19-23

The generations of Eve's daughters
Adam's daughters—Moses 6:11; Genesis 5:4
Seth's daughters—Moses 6:14; Genesis 5:7
Enos's daughters—Moses 6:18; Genesis 5:10
Cainen's daughters—Moses 6:19; Genesis 5:13
Mahalaleel's daughters—Moses 6:20; Genesis 5:16
Jared's daughters—Moses 6:21; Genesis 5:19
Enoch's daughters—Genesis 5:22
Methuselah's daughters—Moses 8:6; Genesis 5:26
Lamech's daughters—Moses 8:10; Genesis 5:30

Noah's wife and Noah's son's wives
Moses 8:12; Genesis 6:18; 7:7, 13; 8:16, 18

Noah's wicked granddaughters
Moses 8:14-15, 21; Genesis 6:1-4

Egyptus, the daughter of Ham and Egyptus
Abraham 1:23-25

Onitah's three daughters
Abraham 1:8, 11-12

Lot's wife
Genesis 14:16; 19:26; Luke 17:32; Abraham 2:4

Lot's daughters
Genesis 14:16; 19:8, 15, 30-38; JST Genesis 19:9-5

Conclusion

Our sisters mentioned in the latter-day scriptures offer a wide spectrum of womanly portraits. Some share remarkable similarities given their differences in time and place. Consider Sariah, who followed her husband into the wilderness, and Emma Smith, who followed her husband from New York to Ohio to Missouri and back to Illinois. Both faced spiritual challenges as well as the hardships of the frontier. Other women mark striking contrasts. Consider the mothers of the stripling warriors, who reared a righteous generation amidst corruption and turmoil, and the daughter of Jared, who corrupted and created turmoil for the generations who followed her. The references may be brief, but the examples are vivid and useful.

Men and women living in our day are fortunate. Because of continuous revelation, Latter-day Saints have more scripture, ancient and modern, than any other Christians in the world. These standard works contain the eternal principles God would have all his children understand and apply. The Apostle Peter knew that, when he listed knowledge along with faith, patience, kindness, and virtue as a necessary attribute of anyone who would gain exaltation. (2 Peter 1:3-9.)

Since no one can be saved in ignorance of the gospel (D&C 131:6), and since one progresses only as fast as he or she gains that knowledge, it follows that the person who takes advantage of the increased number and variety of scriptures available will have "the advantage in the world to come." (D&C 130:18-19.) For many women, identifying the womanly examples in scripture is the first step to becoming a sister scripturian. It is the stories and examples that make the scriptures come alive. The truly successful student is one who can liken and apply the scriptures to herself, and again it is the stories of the struggles and successes of real people that facilitate that application.

More importantly, one must rely on the Spirit, must pray and ponder. Heavenly Father has promised everyone the blessing of knowledge gained "line upon line, precept upon precept" (see 2 Nephi 28:30), but first one must desire that knowledge and seek it diligently.

The truths contained in scripture help one make decisions from an eternal perspective. Today, when modern women's lives are in flux, when the most basic premises of a woman's purpose are under examination, being questioned and challenged, such an eternal perspective takes on increasing importance. The scriptures can give balance to women trying to weigh traditional roles with new opportunities. Knowing the scriptures can give a woman her own light at a time when having the ability to direct her life by her own light is critical.

Fortunately the latter-day scriptures provide examples that are both meaningful and exciting. Discovering those womanly examples can be a joyful experience—delightfully surprising—that is the true beginning of a fuller understanding. With the hope that many will want to embark on that adventure, the following references are offered:

Book of Mormon (References to Women in Order of Appearance)
1 Nephi 1:1 (goodly parents); 2:5; 5:1-10, 11; 7:6, 19; 8:14; 11:13, 15, 18-20; 13:7-8, 17, 34; 14:9-13, 16-17; 16:7, 27, 31, 35-36; 17:1-2, 20, 55; 18:6, 9, 17 (parents), 19; 21:1, 5, 15, 18, 22-23; 22:6, 13-14

2 Nephi 2:18-19, 22-23 ("they" meaning Adam and Eve); 3:1; 4:3-5, 8-9; 5:6; 6:6-7; 7:1; 8:2, 18, 25; 9:21; 10:9, 16; 13:12, 16-24; 14:1, 4; 15:14; 19:17; 20:2, 30, 32; 23:16; 24:2; 26:33; 28:18

Jacob 1:15; 2:7, 24-33, 35; 3:5, 7; 5:54, 56, 60

Mosiah 2:5, 26; 3:8; 5:7; 8:20; 9:2; 10:5, 9; 11:2, 4, 14; 12:29; 13:18,

20, 24; 16:3 (first parents); 18:34; 19:9-24; 20 (the entire chapter is the story of the daughters of the Lamanites); 21:9-10, 17, 20; 22:2, 8; 23:28, 33-34, 38; 24:22; 25:12; 27:25

Alma 1:30; 2:25; 3:1-2, 7; 7:10, 27; 10:11; 11:44; 12:21, 26 (first parents); 14:8-11; 15:2; 17:24; 18:43; 19:2-30; 22:19-24; 23:3 ("household" meaning queen and servants); 24 (entire chapter related to mothers of young stripling warriors); 25:4-9 (related to descendants of kidnapped Lamanite daughters); 27 (entire chapter related to mothers of young stripling warriors); 28:5-6; 30:18; 32:23; 35:14; 39:3-4, 11; 42:2, 7 (first parents); 43:9, 13 (descendants of kidnapped Lamanite daughters), 45; 44:5; 46:12; 47:32-35; 48:10, 24; 50:21, 30-31; 52:12; 53:7 (also most of chapter relates to mothers of stripling warriors); 54:3, 11-12; 55:17; 56 (entire chapter relates to mothers of stripling warriors); 57:21; 58:12, 30-31; 60:17; 63:4-6

Helaman 1:27; 5:6 (first parents); 6:13, 26 (first parents); 11:33; 15:2

3 Nephi 2:12, 16; 3:13; 7:8; 8:25; 9:2, 20 (relates to mothers of stripling warriors); 10:4-6; 12:28, 31-32; 17:10-11 ("they" meaning men and women), 25; 18:21; 19:1; 20:37, 41; 21:16, 18-19 (refers to witchcraft and the forbidden practice of worshiping the fertility goddess); 22:1-8; 24:5; 26:16 (children blessed)

Mormon 1:19; 2:10, 23; 4:14-15, 21; 6:7, 15, 19; 8:40

Ether 1:41 (families); 3:14; 6:3, 15-16, 20; 7:2, 4, 12, 14, 26; 8:1, 4, 8-17, 25 (first parents); 9:2-7, 21, 24-25; 10:2, 5, 14, 16-17, 29; 13:17; 14:2, 17, 22, 31; 15:2, 15, 23 ("they" meaning men and women)

Moroni 9:7-10, 16, 19; 10:31

Doctrine and Covenants (References to Women in Order of Appearance)
10:65; 18:42; 19:25; 20:18-20, 70 ("every member of the church"), 73-74; 21:8; 25 (entire section); 29:2, 21; 33:17 (refers to parable of the ten virgins); 42:22, 80-93; 43:24; 45:56; 49:15-16, 22; 63:14, 16, 54; 64:41-43; 68:25-28 (parents); 74:1; 75:24-28 (families); 76:24; 83 (entire section); 84:27, 101; 85:12 (refers to daughters of Barzillai); 86:3; 88:94, 105; 90:28-31; 97:18-20, 25-28; 98 (entire section speaks of families); 100 (entire section gives assurances to families); 101:81-84; 105:5, 31-34; 109:69-72, 74; 113:8-10; 115:6; 118:3 (families); 122:6; 123:7, 9; 124:6, 11, 61; 126 (entire section refers to Brigham Young's

family); 128:18; 132 (entire section discusses marriage — the new and everlasting covenant); 136:8, 35; 137:5; 138:39

Pearl of Great Price (References to Women in Order of Appearance)
Moses 2:27-28; 3:20, 22-25; 4:6-14, 18-23, 26-27; 5:1-5, 11-12, 16-17, 27-28, 36-37, 41-47, 52-53; 6:2, 9, 11, 14, 18-21; 7:48; 8:6, 10, 12, 14-15, 21

Abraham 1:8, 11-12, 23-25; 2:2, 4, 15, 22-25; 4:27-31; 5:14-21

Joseph Smith–Matthew 16

Joseph Smith–History 4, 7, 20, 41 (reference in Joel is to sons and daughters), 57-58, 61-62, 75

Index

69-70; sealing of, to Joseph
Smith, 69; death of, 70;
summary description of,
70-71
Jaredites: prophets among,
46, 50; succession of kings
among, 49-50
Jaredite daughters: references
to, 45-46
Jared (descendant of first
Jared) conspires with
daughter, 47-48
Jared, wicked daughter of:
suggests seeking secret
combinations, 47, 48;
marries Akish, 48-49
Jared: led family from tower,
11, 46; daughters of, 46
Jeremiah, 2
Jerusalem: wickedness in, in
Lehi's time, 2-3; siege of,
by Nebuchadnezzar, 3
Jesus Christ: speaks to
Nephites from darkness,
42; appearances of, to
Nephites, 42-43, 44;
blesses Nephite children,
43; coming of, foreseen by
Nephite prophets, 43-44;
becoming children of,
44-45; teachings of,
featuring women, 57
John the Baptist, 134-35
Joseph Smith Translation of
the Bible, 134-35, 141
Joseph Smith: moved families
in various treks, 11

Kimball, Heber C., writes of
Vienna Jaques, 65
Kirtland Temple, 98
Korihor, the antichrist, 33

Laban, 3
Lamanites: spare Nephites

because of women's
entreaties, 15; king of,
captured by Limhi's
people, 16; Alma bargains
with, for lives, 18-19; sons
of Mosiah preach to, 22;
beginning of Church
among, 26; women of,
singled out often, 30;
conversion of, due to
courage of Anti-Nephi-
Lehies, 32
Lamanite daughters:
kidnapping of, by wicked
priests, 16-17; moral
strength of, 21
Laman and Lemuel: become
angry and abuse Nephi,
5-6, 9-10; Ishmael's
daughter pleads with, 6;
Lehi despairs over, 6-7;
daughters of, receive
blessing, 9
Lamech, 130-31
Lamoni's queen: exhibits
faith in Ammon, 24; is
overcome by Spirit, 25;
great faith of, 30
Lamoni, father of: encounters
son on road, 27; wife of,
seeks to kill Aaron, 28;
conversion of, 28
Lamoni, King: conversion
and apparent death of,
23-24; Ammon's
conversations with, 23;
rises from "deathbed,"
24-25; conversion of
household of, 25-26
Lehi-Nephi, land of: Nephi
flees to, 13; Zeniff's people
take possession of, 13-14
Lehi: was warned to flee
Jerusalem, 3; sends sons
for brass plates, 3-4;